INTENTION BASED FIELD RESONANCE TESTING

INTENTION BASED FIELD RESONANCE TESTING

The Geometry of the Whisper

STEVEN R TONSAGER

INTENTION BASED FIELD RESONANCE TESTING
The Geometry of the Whisper
© Copyright 2021 Steven R Tonsager

All rights reserved. No part of this book may be used or reproduced in any manner whatsoever without written permission of the author except in the case of brief quotations embodied in critical articles and reviews.

The information in this book is distributed as an "as is" basis, without warranty. Although every precaution has been taken in the preparation of this work, neither the author nor the publisher shall have any liability to any person or entity with respect to any loss or damage caused or alleged to be caused directly or indirectly by the information contained in this book.

First Edition
ISBN: 978-1-946195-98-2

Published by FuzionPress
1250 E 115th Street
Burnsville, MN 55337
FuzionPress.com
612-781-2815

FOREWORD

I first met Steve and Ardith Tonsager 16 years ago. I was a new mother with three young boys who had been in Chiropractic practice for about seven years. I have a son who dealt with food allergies and was referred to Steve as someone that could potentially help. It was amazing to watch Steve work. Each visit came with more knowledge and understanding. I loved my time in his office. The added bonus was the great conversations with his wife, Ardith, who shared his passion and wisdom. I was unaware at the time, but I had embarked on a journey that would become a lifelong friendship and mentorship that would change my life and the life of our patients.

As the years have gone by, we have shared some amazing healing stories together, both with my own family and the family of patients we shared. I have watched first-hand the evolution of Intention Based Field Resonance Testing and whisperology. Steve has shared many concepts and ideas about the theory behind IBFRT and how each person would benefit from care. As a Chiropractor, I had always believed in holistic methods but during my conversations with Steve, I began to fully understand the scope of what that really meant. IBFRT is so much more than simply a treatment, but rather a way to address the incoherencies in their physical, mental, emotional, and spiritual "layers". Almost every conversation ended with a discussion about when he (Steve) was going to teach me IBFRT. It became a regular occurrence and one that was very exciting and intriguing at the same time.

Once the time came for Steve to begin teaching me how to use IBFRT, I was nervous but looked forward to learning with great anticipation. How would I begin to understand something that took decades to develop? Would I be able to utilize the "Geometry of the Whisper"? Over the past 9 months, I have been working with more patients each week; listening and learning. I can now truly appreciate all that Steve has given to his patients, his friends, colleagues, and our communities. Every whisper, remedy, sequence, and incoherence has been treated with pure love and the acknowledgement that we are honoring a life source that is so much greater than ourselves.

I gratefully acknowledge that my purpose is to help people understand their capacity to be well when living a life in congruence with their energy source. I am honored to have been included in this journey and feel blessed to introduce this transformational piece of work. I invite you to learn from Steve as I have. If you allow it to become a part of what you do (and how you live) you will experience the same changes that I have. It is truly a gift from God.

Gina R. Cleveland, D.C.

FOREWORD
A MIGHTY WHISPER

Medicine is continually under tension to give causes for the diseases with which it deals. Indeed, comprehensive theories and explanations for human ailments are the most venerable and willing fixation of the profession. In the West, for example, the theory that the circulation of bodily humors among organs produced and determined the course of illnesses was accepted. For centuries medicine tried to intervene with bloodletting, leeching, and purging.

Fast forward to the 1930s, and the entry of antibiotics revolutionized medicine. Penicillin and sulfonamides treated a significant number of infectious diseases that had frequently been lethal. Cures were now available provided one knew sufficiently about the underlying pathogen and its mechanism. Almost overnight, doctors became enthusiasts and optimists. This period is often ascribed as the beginning of modern medicine. Looking back, it was a major triumph for medical science but perhaps not a revolution after all. The actual revolution in medicine, which prepared the way for antibiotics and other useful treatments, occurred a century before penicillin. This revolution began in the 1830s with the *destruction of dogma*. It was discovered that much of medicine was nonsense.

Gradually, the "art of medicine" emerged. In hindsight, this art was the starting point of the science of medicine. It was based on thorough and careful examinations of sick people. Correct diagnosis became the principal aim of medicine. As diagnostic methods evolved, disease prognosis became possible. Doctors could, with some dependability, tell their patients about the outcomes of their illness. In the 21st century, these are usually accepted as the primary responsibilities of the physician.

The art of medicine has been dominated and even canceled out by computers and a deluge of information in ever-growing protocols, algorithms, and guidelines, all supposed to make the job easier and safer for doctors. Yet, for all the technology, it seems to me the one hard scientific truth is that we are profoundly ignorant about nature and human capacities. The depth and scope of our ignorance represent a challenge to human intellect. Our simple-minded I-know-it-all approach is no match for the complexity of existence. We are getting glimpses of how monumental the questions are and how much we still have to learn.

I believe there are essential questions to ask. Is there a limit to scientific inquiry not set by what is knowable but by what we ought to be knowing? Are there some types of information that serve as a lens to the real cause of dis-ease? My own intuition gives me a resounding yes. Answers can do no more than respond to the limits of any question and context. Medicine is limited by ignoring the context entirely. Instead, it looks for answers in the content of data. We quickly become slaves to narrow data information via medical technology. We have lost something sacred about the patient-doctor communication and relationship, imprisoned by an invisible cage to separation, fragmentation, and compartmentalization.

My own dissatisfaction with modern medicine's pursuits to figure out and treat immune diseases with only biochemistry was a catalyst in my decision to visit Steve Tonsager at his clinic in River Falls, Wisconsin. I hoped Tonsager had something up his sleeve. Some medical marvel. Unassuming, without badges and honors, Tonsager is healer par excellence. His clinic rule is "speak your mind." I could explore freely, speak my story. What appeared to be a single hour was really two. Deep listening and quiet integrity exuded out of him. Diving deeply into possible connections while carefully muscle testing my ankles, he drew information from a reality reaching beyond what is immediately before him. He had access to the invisible fields. I appreciated being shown another side of a physical issue.

Tonsager shows that our stories survive because they provide guidance in dealing with uncertainty and the unavoidable unknown. Evolution is tied to the experience of the chaos of illness. It helps to explain the profound psychological appeal of our inner beliefs and the stories we tell ourselves. Above all, he alerts his clients to topics rarely discussed at the bedside: "set your inner house in order," and Tonsager provides practical advice on doing this. He is, in fact, addressing questions of concern to everyone. Foremost is that you must take responsibility for your own life. Period.

One could not but be struck by another unusual thing about Tonsager: Here was a healer who had given himself a great spiritual education. He not only loves and respects the physicist, Dr. William Tiller, but also medical doctor and mystic, David Hawkins, and treats them both as his most treasured friends. One of the book's many virtues is that it provides an entry point into Map of Consciousness, a hugely complex work. Tonsager worked out his approach to whisperology with Dr. David Hawkins' discoveries into the scope of human consciousness as a foundation. It is foundational because no matter how different our genes or life experiences may be, we all have to handle the unknown. Whisperology gives us a path to move from chaos to coherence.

It became clear that thinking through a problem was, for him, a process of filtering all necessary information and elements of an organ or tissue. An original healer, Tonsager cares about a thought only if it might, in some way, be helpful to someone. The brilliance of this book is his demonstration of how every healing encounter is preceded by an intentional thought. The intention is the central, organizing theme throughout the book. It can be the first principle in one's life. By intention, one can send and receive information through the powers of attention, attraction, and intention.

In Tonsager's unique approach, his intention is sent forth and accelerated by whispering in a highly-skilled way, taking in all the numberless tons of factors of an ailment. Whispering is strong enough to support the full weight of the mind that thought up heart transplants, joint replacements, and the mighty drug industry. Whispering is the joining of man's deep-rooted capacity with the special prerogative of the Divine; this is a very special form of communication. Relating to circumstances for an event and how it can be fully understood and assessed, the context of a whisper is investigated.

In his overarching whisperology, Tonsager's discoveries have opened up a new vista for information assembling: The Figure - a group of seven major isosceles triangles with nine smaller triangles contained within each major one. Imagine The Figure to be an encampment in the desert. Take a seat. There is enough space for you. It's dusk in the land of a healing period. What's happening? Who's going to stand up and whisper? In the healing ritual, The Figure is persuaded to release information in the specific *triangle containing the incoherence* via a powerful whisper. We watch the space within the target triangle shift to a more coherent, more ordered, and healthy state. The target, be it an organ like the kidney, a cell in your eye, a narrowed blood vessel, a long-forgotten motor accident, or an emotionally charged divorce percolating in one's soul. The arrangement and shape, symmetry, and patterns with The Figure are not unlike the structure of crystals. Viewed in this way, every chaos consists, it seems, of a characteristic arrangement within it, a visual marker of Tonsager's earnest quest to move beyond simplistic cause-effect. The Figure's sixty-three triangles exist at the interface between the visible matter and non-physical invisible realms.

The Figure bears a relationship to the organization of physical organs, the human experience of temporal events, and spiritual values. The geometry of The Figure, based on Map of Consciousness, has an element of universality. The intimacy between a human and belief patterns can be so long-standing that a form of molecular crystallization becomes possible. Putting together new combinations of medicines is simply not up to the job. Clients continue to pour in to see Tonsager, have kept listening for Steve's whispers because what he is saying meets a deep and unarticulated need. The geometry of the whisper has the accuracy and precision of a surgeon. Exactly how the mind would accomplish this with precision, with, say, shoulder pain and leave all else alone, I couldn't figure it out. Still, I am satisfied to leave it there anyhow.

It is also a wonderful problem in need of solving. Just think what we would know if we had anything like a clear understanding of what goes on when whisperology vanishes pain away. Best of all, we would find out about the superintelligence that exists in each of us, boundlessly more brilliant and possessing technical know-how far beyond our present understanding. It would be worth a National Institute of Whisperology.

The great need now, for the medicine of the future, is for more information at the most fundamental levels of the living process. We are creating a beginning, and there ought to be some satisfaction, even excitement, in that. The whiperology method works. It follows from this that it is now possible to begin thinking about a human society relatively free of disease. This would indeed have been an inconceivable notion a half-century ago, and oddly enough, it has a rather revolutionary sound today. Heart attacks and strokes, cancer, and rheumatoid arthritis are not natural features of the human condition. We must rid ourselves of such impediments as quickly as we can.

Tonsager's wonderful and unique spouse, Ardith, was all in; she embraced and encouraged her husband's unique healing gifts. They both displayed courage and continue to live by the highest intention, some of which can be very demanding. I saw Tonsager grow, from the remarkable person he was, into someone even more able and assured— through intention and spiritual work. He shows how each individual has the ultimate responsibility to bear; to live a full life, one first sets one's own house in order with intention. Only then can one reasonably take on all the grandeur life offers.

Gloria in Excelsis Deo!

Dr. Nisha J. Manek, MD, FACP, is the author of *Bridging Science and Spirit: The Genius of William A. Tiller's Physics and the Promise of Information Medicine*

ACKNOWLEDGEMENTS

I want to thank Dr. Nisha Manek for her thoughtful insights and brilliance as it relates to the material in this book. I also want to thank Dr. Gina Cleveland for her kind words and reflection of someone extremely skilled practicing the teachings presented in this material.

Huge thank you to my patients and students for the opportunity to be a part of their lives and their journeys toward true coherence with themselves and others.

A special thank you to my business partner and a dear friend, Jasna Burza, for helping me bring this work into the world.

I have Ardith to thank for her inspiration and powerful analysis of the applicability and intelligibility of this material. In a previous book, I referred to the vastness of her love and friendship as "the land of Ardith." I believe that I still reside in this land and that she continues to watch over me and guide me.

TABLE OF CONTENTS

INTRODUCTION. The Expansion of the Toolbox	17
THE ORIGIN OF WHISPEROLOGY	26
PART I. THE NEW TOOL	61
CHAPTER ONE	63
Introducing the new tool	63
The First Question: Why did you choose a triangle?	63
The Second Question: What has a triangle to do with consciousness, science, and healing?	68
A Unified Theory	69
CHAPTER TWO	73
Tool design and composition	73
Tool design	74
Tool composition	76
A New Antenna	77
Where does the tool come from?	80
CHAPTER THREE	83
Contextual space and coherence	83
Contextual space	83
Seven Primary Contextual Spaces	85
Context Heals Content	88
Stress and Incoherence	91
All Space is Connected	92

PART II. TOOL APPLICATION	95
CHAPTER FOUR	97
Core Beliefs and Guiding Principles	97
Tool Maximization	98
Elemental Coherence	102
Subdivision of triangles	104
Deltopes	107
CHAPTER FIVE	111
The Seven Primary Triangles	111
Alignment with the Eternal Aspect	128
CHAPTER SIX	133
The First Use of the Tool	133
Example One. Physical Trauma	137
Additional Comments about Example One	143
Example Two. Iatrogenic Effects	145
Additional Comments About Example Two	147
CHAPTER SEVEN	151
The Second Use of the Tool	151
Example Three. A Life Changing Accident	157
Additional Comments about Example Three	159
CONCLUSION. The Evolution of Whisperology	163
APPENDIX	
Meditation	173
Figures	175
Glossary	183
Suggested Reading	189

INTRODUCTION
The Expansion of the Toolbox

What is the geometry of the whisper? The geometry of the whisper is an exciting expansion of the theory and application of whisperology. For those of you who have not read my previous books, the term *whisperology* may appear strange or silly. The study and practice of whisperology includes consideration of the following elements to describe the power and efficacy of intention: consciousness, information, energy, form, and space. Each of these elements are integral to the development of the theories and methods that comprise my current work, called Intention Based Field Resonance Testing (IBFRT).

I think it is helpful to try to explain how whisperology has come into existence and evolved over time. You are encouraged to read the five books in the order of their creation to gain a better sense of what I mean by whisperology.

The first book, *The Powers of Attention, Attraction, and Intention in Field Control Therapy: My Pathway of Adventure, Discovery, and Healing: A Practitioner's Perspective*, was written to expand the scope and application of field control therapy (FCT) to its practitioners and those interested in treatment of a range of problems through novel means. I described it this way:

"FCT is an adventure—not only a means of helping others, but a door to self-discovery. New perspectives emerge that not only are healing to a patient, but to us, as well. New ideas about what is actually occurring in the testing and treatment processes are invited and come to the surface for investigation and reflection. This adventure has led me to new insights and applications that have benefited many patients."[1]

In the second book, *Intention Based Field Resonance Testing: The Power of the Whisper*, the anatomy and efficacy of the whisper are described. The power of the whisper is based on the interaction between intention and its target to create changes that benefit health on many different levels—including the spiritual, mental, emotional, and physical planes. I described the emerging concepts and applications of whisperology as a response to being invited by the Divine to follow my own path:

"To simplify and move forward in my life, I have ventured into my own methods of imprinting information into vials and in many situations eliminated the need to use anything complicated to get the messages into the bottles. Sometimes, just whispering is a lot easier, and perhaps even better. Sometimes I just forgo the bottle and start whispering!"[2]

"Every whisper is preceded by a thought, an intention. This is a central, organizing theme throughout the book and has become the first principle in my professional and personal life."[3]

---

[1] Tonsager, Steven R, *The Powers of Attention, Attraction, and Intention in Field Control Therapy* (Dog Ear Publishing, Indianapolis, IN: 2015) p. xi
[2] Tonsager, Steven R. *Intention Based Field Resonance Testing: The Power of the Whisper* (Dog Ear Publishing, Indianapolis, IN: 2016) p. 3.
[3] Ibid.

"I continue to be fascinated by the ability—which we mostly don't realize we have been given by the Creator, the source of life—to affect our own health, and the health of others through our whispering."[4]

"Over the next few hundred years, healing through intention (information medicine) will become the dominant way to restore and enhance health... there are still relatively few of us who know how, and even trust that it is possible, to whisper to human beings in such a way that current concepts of disease are way too small for us."[5]

In the third book, *Intention Based Field Resonance Testing: The Magnification of the Whisper*, the volume and accuracy of the whisper is explored. The context for this book was:

In my first book, the term *whisperology* was not used overtly, although there were many indirect references to a new way of sending and receiving information through the powers of attention, attraction, and intention. The term *whisperology* was introduced in the second book specifically to express the underlying conceptual framework of what I described as Intention Based Field Resonance Testing (IBFRT). Whisperology became my way of describing to others my new methods and wonderful outcomes, in a fashion that was both serious and light-hearted."[6]

'In this book, we will explore how the anatomy of a whisper provides a basis for magnifying the whisper's power."[7]

"The cultivation of intention through spiritual work is central to all of the new developments."[8]

---

[4] Ibid, p. 4

[5] Ibid, p. 5

[6] Tonsager, Steven R. *Intention Based Field Resonance Testing: The Magnification of the Whisper* (Dog Ear Publishing, Indianapolis, IN: 2017) p. 1.

[7] Ibid.

[8] Ibid, p. 2

"The tool introduced in this current book utilizes numbers. Sequences of numbers are like codes, informational keys, or even a language able to communicate with human information systems... The inclusion of numerical sequences in IBFRT marks the beginning of a new stage in the intention-based conceptual realm, with new applications and exciting results."[9]

Through the use of numerical sequences, intention is focused on a very precise target with the additional benefit that the numerical sequences can be used by someone besides the person that initiated the intention, the "whisper." The common language of numerical symbols unifies and intensifies the power of intention, by combining the whispering activities of more than one person, to create additional coherency and magnification of effort. The numerical sequences can be shared with others to add precision to the intention and the accuracy of finding the target.

During the time that I was writing the second and third books, I wrote the outlines and developed the allegories for two other books. I especially enjoyed writing these stories and hoped that a different approach, allegories, would prove to be helpful regarding the importance of developing a personal spiritual discipline of prayer and meditation. There is a great deal of emphasis in all of my books about the importance of spiritual drills and the essential role spiritual work plays in the practice of whisperology. *The Dreams of EBKILFGN, An Allegory About Consciousness* and *The Tales of EBKILFGN: An Allegory About Enlightenment*, add to the resources that the reader may access to put their own spiritual work and understanding in a new context.

In this latest book, *Intention Based Field Resonance Testing: The Geometry of the Whisper,* the *context* of the whisper is investigated. The geometry of the whisper is reflective of a spatial network that connects the potential of a whisper with its actualization. The space describes a

---

[9] Ibid, p. 3

primary structure that is of triangular shape. Like a file cabinet that contains information within certain folders that are sorted alphabetically, the geometry of the whisper is an organizational structure that identifies the location of a whisper. These structures are virtual spaces through which intention is manifested in the physical world.

About a year after I began working on the geometry of the whisper, my friend Bill Tiller asked me to write another book to explain these new developments so he could study it. We had been discussing the topic every couple of months. I told Bill that I was not finished with the work but promised I would send him the sections that were partially completed. A few weeks later, when Ardith and I were visiting Bill and his wife Jean at their home, I asked him if it helped to read the first part of the manuscript. Bill told me that he didn't understand it. Bill said that he knew that I was "on to something and that it fit with his own work of imprinting and broadcasting intention" but the manuscript was confusing not clarifying.

I pulled out a couple of the triangular diagrams from the manuscript I sent him, and described how I use the diagrams with the patients in the clinic. I described the relationship between the triangles and the other whisperology tools. Bill told me that when I explained it to him in this way, it made sense. One of the benefits of our conversation was a renewed appreciation of the difficulty to write something that is much easier to experience, or to demonstrate, in person, than to explain with words. I also reminded Bill that not only did the book itself need more work, there was further investigation that I needed to do to comprehend more deeply the geometry of a whisper.

Obviously, I hope that the book in its present and significantly revised form will be intelligible to the reader. I am also aware that whisperology is not for everyone. Many possible obstacles await the reader which are best appreciated as *contextual land mines*. The spatial tool that will be introduced in this book has a home in the material and spiritual world. Or, perhaps a better way of stating it is to suggest that the tool exists at the interface between the physical and non-physical domains, or the doorway between linear and non-linear levels of consciousness.

Most people will struggle to comprehend and value the distinction between the world they know, *as they perceive it*, and an invisible world within, or beyond, the physical world. Not a world of things that are simply too small to see, but a domain that is of an entirely different dimension, known only in past centuries by very few people through spiritual work and subjective experience. These enlightened ones were given the gift of spiritual vision, sometimes called the opening of the third eye, which transformed the context of life and transcended the perception of duality between subject and object in the so-called real world of space time.

The expanded context in which subject and object no longer exist as separate entities presents a nearly insurmountable barrier to scientific theory and religious doctrine because passing through the barrier requires the surrender of what each group believes to be objectively true. This is a powerful reason to explain why the geometry of the whisper will not conform with what is accepted as fact, or gospel; what is offered here will be neither sufficiently scientific nor religious to meet the conventionally accepted standards of truth and its verification. For both sides, the word *dogma* captures the attitude of entrenchment about what is known, *or believed*, to be the fundamental and non-negotiable framework to understand the relationship between the human being and the rest of creation. With so much effort and significant investment of resources to strengthen the fortresses of science and religion, it should not be surprising that fierce resistance is encountered by anyone who would find the fortress to be fragile, not impenetrable.

Nonetheless, I offer the geometry of the whisper with the hope that it may be of value to someone in the present and future. I do not intend to offend anyone who finds that the current structure in which he or she resides to be satisfactory, even perfect. However, from a different context, a different *positionality*, that will be described in this volume, the fortress does not appear to be too different from any other building.

Every breakthrough in understanding requires letting go of something that is familiar. More coherent answers are found by exploring a larger context, not through the rearrangement or elaboration of content within an unchanging context. The disagreements about content, whether it be in the scientific or religious community, typically ignore the lack of a common context between opposing viewpoints and institutions. David Hawkins offered great clarity about the critical distinction between content and context in his books which I highly recommend to my patients, and to all of you.

The geometry of the whisper introduces a tool that comes from a context, a level of consciousness, that is outside time and space. In this realm there are nonlinear governing laws that are not directly accessible to the linear methods of science. Spiritual laws are only accessible through subjective truth and experience. There will be many readers who will struggle with the contents of this book because the context of their lives—including religious experience—orients them to a transcendent God not an imminent divine presence. The tension between religious groups has been present for centuries, exemplified in the ways of the mystic that often were at odds with the traditional teachings. It is probably safe to say that I will manage to offend, or not be taken seriously, by both scientifically and religiously minded readers with the new book.

Bill Tiller is fond of saying that we are spiritual beings having a physical experience. I think his conceptualization of a human being, *and the human experience,* provides a compelling resolution to many of the difficulties for science or religion because the context has been expanded. Bill's research reflects the work of a scientist and a mystic with a highly evolved level of consciousness. I believe his most important discoveries about the nature of consciousness and the power of intention to change physical space would not have been possible without his and Jean's meditative practice.

Like many others, I have been blessed by the opportunity to study the writings of others and learn from many kinds of teachers. However, what has encouraged me the most is the evolution of consciousness that takes place *through doing my own spiritual work*. No one can do it for you! The importance of practicing a spiritual discipline was discussed in *Intention Based Field Resonance Testing: The Power of the Whisper*. I found the encouragement to become more serious about these practices in the writings of David Hawkins and Bill Tiller, as well as the freedom to create the drills that would help me to grow. In space time, the gold standard is the reliable outcome, or effect, which is produced by a cause that is not influenced by the person who initiates or monitors the result. The belief system is considered to be objective. However, in an expanded frame of reference that is not defined by space time, the gold standard is left behind because the limitations of duality are overcome. From a higher positionality, everything, including every aspect of what it means to be human, is subject to what is held in consciousness.

In Chapter 7 of the last book of his trilogy, *I. Reality and Subjectivity*, Hawkins answers questions about the relationship between a teacher and student. He writes, "Many spiritual students are widely read and already mentally know about many spiritual truths, but the information is stored in the memory of the mental body only and thus awaits activation by the actual presence of a teacher in whom those higher spiritual bodies are highly energized."[10]

Hawkins is asked a follow-up question. "Q: Is the student's comprehension then dependent upon the teacher's level of consciousness?"[11]

---

[10] Hawkins, David R. *I Reality And Subjectivity* (Veritas Press, Sedona, Arizona: 2003) p. 134
[11] Ibid, p. 135

He replies, "A: The comprehension is based on the effect of the Se. or represented by willingness, openness, intention, and the level of consciousness of the listener as well as that of the teacher. It is a common, everyday experience for people to know something but many years may elapse before they suddenly 'get' it. This readiness is often a consequence of periods of reflection, contemplation, prayer, and karmic potential."[12]

I am indebted to David Hawkins and Bill Tiller because each of them in his own way, helped me to finally get it. I hope that my books will be a catalyst for you to also experience your own epiphany. I am going to imagine as you are reading this book, that I am beside you, like I was with my friend Bill, doing the best I can to explain how the newest tool in whisperology has helped many people with their troubles, whether the difficulties are physical, emotional, mental, spiritual, or, all of the above. I look forward to sharing with you, dear reader, the new tool, that has helped me to whisper with greater wisdom and understanding. Perhaps you might appreciate why I categorize the new tool of whisperology as a *contextual tool*.

A contextual tool does not fit into the toolbox of a materialist. In the space time world, any person can pick up a hammer, and with varying degrees of skill, use it to drive a nail into a piece of wood. Yes, the activity of hammering a nail is plain for all to see. In the world of whisperology, a hammer is only a hammer for the person who has done the necessary spiritual work to pick up the invisible tool and cooperate with its inherent purpose to simply manifest its essence.

---

[12] Ibid.

The Origin of Whisperology

The evolution of whisperology is an intriguing story—at least it is for me! Based on conversations with people who have read my books, lay and professional, not everyone has found the reading to be easy. Interesting? Yes. Strange? Absolutely. Credible? Maybe. Therefore, I decided to begin this book by including passages from the other books that include key concepts and findings about whisperology. I think this will be very helpful for the comprehension of this book about whisper geometry. The reader may decide to read the other books if some of the passages are sufficiently persuasive that the effort is worth the time.

FIRST BOOK

The first book, *The Powers of Attention, Attraction, and Intention in Field Control Therapy, My Pathway of Adventure, Discovery, and Healing: A Practitioner's Perspective*, was written to expand the scope and application of FCT to its practitioners and those interested in treatment of a range of problems through novel means. Throughout the book, I offered practical advice to make the theory and application of FCT more understandable to patients through analogies and AK (Applied Kinesiology) demonstrations using examples of possible conversations with patients unfamiliar to FCT.

Early in the book, beginning in Chapter 2, the potential for a qualitatively different context into which bio-resonance testing might be placed was introduced into the discussion. I referred to these developments as "upgrades of my mental software."[13] I wrote:

"Consider the possibility that there are important qualities and larger contexts into which the FCT model can be expanded beyond the

---

[13] Tonsager, *The Powers of Attention, Attraction, and Intention in Field Control Therapy*, p.17.

present scope. We have an ability to do this with the tool called intention—'our own personal mouse' as I like to refer to it. Intention combined with attention to undiscovered (but discoverable) information offers you a one-way ticket to a place or a new attraction that you may have never visited before... It offers you the opportunity to set aside any limiting beliefs about health, both how to identify and treat any negative influences and how to encourage greater health of body, mind, soul, and spirit."[14]

Given the applicability of the power of intention to explore new territory, I carefully examined the FCT theories and applications through my mental software. I eventually came to the conclusion that "a potentially limiting belief system... is that all of the necessary information about a certain organ, tissue, or pathogen is to be found in its corresponding filter. The belief continues that when a remedy is made using this particular filter, it will provide all the relevant elements concerning the meaning of the filter. This is a belief system that is reinforced in the testing process, when the filter is used to generate a response measured by the tester. It is likely that this belief is held in mind, and therefore the practitioner is subject to it. As others have often said, 'We are subject to what we hold in mind.' Therefore, the interpretation of a stress response or lack of a response concerning any one of the FCT moves is also an exercise that reinforces the FCT belief system."[15]

Now that I had begun the process of exploring the tenets of FCT from my perspective, other questions about the comprehensiveness of the filters came to mind which led me to further explore the nature of the filters themselves. "I discovered that every organizing filter could be represented by a number..."[16] At that time, I set aside some of my findings about the numbers until the topic of numerical sequences as a tool of whisperology became the focus of later work that is shared in

---

[14] Ibid.
[15] Ibid.
[16] Ibid, p. 19

the third book. "My intuition encouraged me to think that there might be other categories or criteria, than the FCT guiding filters to describe the obstacles toward improved health—and not just from a physical perspective."[17] I referred to this exploration as "swimming outside the markers" of FCT to search for additional relevant information.[18]

I wanted to bring the mental software "upgrades" into day-to-day activities. I created a different style of interactive conversation with patients to enlist their cooperation to uncover other relevant information about their health, including time and location. This improved the accuracy of finding stressed or diseased areas, sources of non-physical stress, and when these events became important. Listening for relevance and accuracy of information was done through learning to use my hands as a point of contact with the patient's feet—a kind of truth and relevance detector! New findings eventually were linked to other scales that distinguished between a physical and non-physical problem. This attenuation of what was at the core of the problem is referred to as "Finding the Bull's-Eye." These strategies are the themes of Chapter 2, Modifications of Testing Procedures.[19] These new concepts and strategies were applied to patients with toxin associated problems.

A major event that took place during this period concerned new methods of creating and delivering remedies, including the use of cold laser as a delivery system which led to a white paper with Dr. Bill Tiller called "Importance of a Coherent Delivery System for Homeopathic Remedies" (White Paper XVII) about information entanglement. Ardith and I first met Dr. Tiller at a holistic dental conference in Arizona in 2009. I had read some of Dr. Tiller's books and articles because his theories were part of the content of FCT theories. Little did I realize that Bill and Jean would become dear friends and a part of a very small

---

[17] Ibid, p. 21
[18] Ibid, p. 22
[19] Ibid, pp. 17-43.

group of people who understood and encouraged me in my work, especially when my findings took me in a different direction than FCT.

I sent Bill the findings about the use of the cold laser in connection with treating a woman with shingles. Bill found my treatment to be an interesting example of his theories regarding intention and information entanglement. Sometime later, I learned from Bill that he asked a doctor named Nisha Manek, who was being mentored by him in Tillerian physics, if she knew anything about me. You might say that she "vetted" me. Why? Because a few years prior to her coming to Arizona, she had come to see me for help with a health issue. Her experience was very positive and powerful. I remember how intrigued she was by the bio-resonance testing. When she asked me to suggest resources for her to become more acquainted with my work, I mentioned the two names that were of greatest influence in my thinking. That was a simple question to answer: Dr. Bill Tiller and Dr. David Hawkins. Obviously, she became more than mildly interested! Bill eventually gave her the task of putting his work into a form that it could be shared with a larger audience. Recently, Dr. Manek wrote a very helpful book about Tillerian physics. Nisha plans to write additional books about Bill's work. Ardith and I are blessed by her support and friendship.

Chapter 5 described several new ways to use MEMON transformers, devices which mitigate the stressful effects of electromagnetic fields from technology, in order to improve patient health and increase coherence. The new approaches to testing expanded the application of MEMON transformers to other health concerns. The list of applications has grown since the publication of the first book.

In Chapter 6, "New Frontiers: The Birth of the H Vial," the reader was introduced to the works of Dr. David Hawkins and the Map of Consciousness. The value of his map for calibrating patients, testing procedures, and increasing efficacy of treatments was introduced. The crucial role of the spiritual growth of the tester was introduced, a major theme of the second book. The link between spiritual growth and testing was described with statements like:

"We are limited only by our own imaginations and contextual fields about what may be understood differently or recontextualized."[20]

"I do not believe I would have been capable of doing this work without working on myself."[21]

Another major development occurred regarding the imprinting process when "I found that I could imprint my Boston amber round vials with a highly coherent field through intention. I could imprint them with a specific meaning concerning a toxin, bacteria, emotion, tissue, or other subject solely by intention. I found that I could imprint these vials with some kind of information that was of very high calibration and gauge the symmetry state."[22] "Intention was required to add or transform the words into a useful diagnostic filter or remedy. I believe that my spiritual work enabled me to uncover and express this ability or gift in the clinic, and perhaps every person has the innate ability to do the very same thing."[23]

I decided to call these vials, H vials, "To honor the inspiration that I received from Dr. David Hawkins."[24] I defined an H vial as follows:

An H vial "is my designation for a filter that has been created for a specific organ, tissue, pathogenic factor, or concept without the use of a substance (made by intention).[25]

I continued to explore what was possible if testing was primarily an expression of human intention. Dr. Tiller discussed how in certain instances the tester became the testing tool which encouraged me to apply his insight to my own experiences with FCT. "In FCT testing, the

---

[20] Ibid, p. 96
[21] Ibid.
[22] Ibid.
[23] Ibid.
[24] Ibid.
[25] Ibid, p. 121

patient holds a metal bar that is connected by a wire to a metal testing platform, and information in the form of homeopathic filters is introduced to see if it elicits a response."[26] (a fairly well-known phenomena known as hemi-body shortening). I asked myself, "Which part of this is essential? Which tool?" Eventually, I found that I could experience the same responses from patients without the apparatus."[27] This was my confirmation of what Bill had said about other testing equipment and the interaction of the tester's intention with the one being tested in what he called conditioned space. Bill referred to these as training wheels.

Once the cat was let out of the bag, there were more interesting findings. "I also found that the remedy could be delivered through an H vial, a vial that was never in contact with a homeopathically created remedy. How was it created? Through intent—through an H vial. Thus, the H vial was born... According to my testing, The H vials also affected the physical world, not unlike Bill Tiller's experiments with intention that are described in his books. I wondered what it was about my intent that created the necessary information and delivery system, which was not unlike the laser that I used in my earlier experiments."[28]

I returned to my growing belief that the most important qualities were carried by the consciousness of the person who intended to help another person. I concluded, "With God's help and guidance, intention is my mouse and will take me wherever I want to go, always with permission, and create what might be helpful for someone else. These findings also encourage me to explore differences between specific and general intent, detailed and general informational content, and different ways of representing the information. The intent is always to honor the source of any information and to only seek information that honors the

---

[26] Ibid, p. 97
[27] Ibid.
[28] Ibid, pp. 97-98

Source in someone else... It is about what is in your heart, no matter how smart or experienced you are."[29]

When I look back at these initial discoveries, I can see I was only getting started. Now my mind was devising new ways to recognize what I was feeling through my hands in the testing as well as what was being imprinted into the vials and my patients. I wrote, "Scales of stress were developed by yours truly, and they were investigated through the H vials, created via intention, for the purpose of identifying and quantifying various stresses or imbalances, including hypertension, acute and chronic pain, susceptibility to allergies, EMF sensitivity, Schumann resonance stress, the largest bio-field distortion, sleep disturbance, anxiety, etc. Dear reader, I'm telling you that I can make a remedy for almost anything... okay, maybe everything."[30]

Source Energy vials are introduced as another new frontier in the last chapter. I defined a Source Energy vial as "A vial that I have created through intent." The intent of this vial is echoed in the meditation toward the end of my book. The intent that is imprinted may be general or very specific, with a particular intention for a particular patient. The use of the term *Source Energy* is intended to designate that the qualities placed into the vial are not personal, but a reflection of certain universal qualities that all human beings share."[31]

Tiller's theories about conditioned space and his hypothesized substance which he called deltrons changed the qualities of physical space to allow for its enhancement through subtle energies invited more questions and explorations. "The paper encouraged me to keep thinking about how I could share my intentions for health of body, mind, soul, and spirit with others. Could it be embedded somehow in a vial? How specific could it be? Was it better to be not so specific? What about the space in the clinic where I meditated every morning, resulting many

---

[29] Ibid.
[30] Ibid, p. 99
[31] Ibid, p. 123

times in me believing I was in a meditative state for most of the day? Was this space also conditioned as described by Dr. Tiller in several of his papers? Was this the reason, or part of the reason, that many patients told me how calm it was in that room?"[32] Bill's work was the catalyst for exploring the creation and use of Source Energy vials.

These questions led to several exciting answers. "Holding vials in my hand while meditating came first. It worked. I found that a vial that was conditioned in this way could be left near an unconditioned vial, and that vial, by the next morning (perhaps earlier), would be conditioned like the first. I found that I could condition a vial that was wrapped in aluminum foil, and that the patient experienced the same effects with a wrapped vial... superluminal fields, yes!"[33] I remember stimulating conversations with Bill and Jean in their home about superluminal phenomena and the subject of deltron coupling.

I studied Bill's theories about conditioned space and non-local effects. His ideas and personal encouragement helped me to explore these matters in my own way back in Wisconsin which I shared in the book. "Eventually I found that I did not need to hold the vial, but that I could place my hands on each side of the vial, my hands a few feet apart, while I meditated and could produce the conditioned vial."[34] "I found that by placing several boxes of vials on my testing table and meditating with my hands around all of them, all vials were conditioned."[35] "I found that I did not need to use my hands. I could simply focus on conditioning the vials."[36] "I found that I could condition the space or air within the vial and achieve the same effect, was more easily done if I held the vial in my hand while meditating."[37] "I found that if I conditioned a vial that

---

[32] Ibid, p. 100
[33] Ibid, p. 101
[34] Ibid.
[35] Ibid.
[36] Ibid.
[37] Ibid.

contained the MEMON water (although it probably doesn't need to be MEMON-conditioned water at all), I could take a small amount of water from the vial that I'd conditioned and transfer it to an unconditioned vial or a larger container of water and the unconditioned vial or larger container acquired the same conditioned quality."[38] "I found that vials made in this way could be taken to other locations or other homes and that the space became conditioned to a more coherent state."[39]

These experiments highlighted the centrality of "Source-centric thinking" and my interest in Source Energy vials. "If something was being altered in my space or within the space of the vial or within me, then it was not about me personally. It was my connection to my Source, to God, and the effects were the manifestation of the energy of the Source."[40] "I believe that the Source has potentized my intention, expanding or perhaps opening my consciousness so that I can be a conduit of some kind to benefit others. I think this is a consequence of my spiritual work and attests to the powers of attention, attraction, and intention!"[41]

I wanted to apply these findings to my patients. "Answers can do no more than respond to the limits of any question and context. My current thought is that if the patient is evaluated for the type of incoherencies that are most relevant and can be addressed, a more specific intention (or intention statement) can be delivered to the vial for the person and for the particular incoherency that can be addressed at the present time. Always ask permission so that there is alignment with the Divine Will."[42] The patient's state of mind is also a relevant aspect of this experience. What do I mean? I developed H vials for different types of incoherency: Physical, emotional, mental, and spiritual. Each type of

---

[38] Ibid.
[39] Ibid, pp. 101-102
[40] Ibid.
[41] Ibid.
[42] Ibid, p. 104

incoherency is affected by the Source Energy vial, and their calibration with the Map of Consciousness is also temporarily raised."[43] "Another very interesting finding was that an intention vial made specifically for one person would not generate the same findings in another person."[44]

I had a powerful sense of being invited by God to keep moving forward, aptly described by the subtitle of the book: *My Pathway of Adventure, Discovery, and Healing: A Practitioner's Perspective.* "The courage to let go of our special exemptions to remain small and special opens the doors to no longer being wedded to an outcome. How does the saying go? 'Father, forgive them, for they know not what they do.' Father, forgive them, for they are clueless. In my moments of cluelessness (you may wonder if I'm going for the record), I find peace in the context of my life, for it shapes and defines the content. I am light, and all I see is light, for behind every appearance, including my own, there is only light. The courage to surrender that which holds us back and our investment in an outcome allows us to be in the moment and truly present, willing to learn and expand our consciousness according to the will and divine intention of our Source. What did Jesus say about faith even the size of a mustard seed?"[45] "As for me, I believe that everything is permeated by the Source energy that originates from a much higher and timeless space and placeless place. Yes, all is made in the image of God. Everything is occurring or unfolding perfectly in its accorded time or karma, and that is good enough for me."[46]

My first book may be viewed as a book of transition. My FCT adventures encouraged the expansion of its theory and methods to explore new territory in an expanded context which is based upon the consciousness of the one who seeks something even more fundamental. I quickly

---

[43] Ibid, p. 106
[44] Ibid, p. 105
[45] Ibid, pp. 107-108
[46] Ibid.

realized that my journey brought me to a very different place than the one described by Dr. Savely Yurkovsky, the inventor of Field Control Therapy, who rejected my early attempts to share my discoveries and conclusions with him as pseudoscience. I expressed to him, and in this book, my gratitude for his work but also stated that my work was not an exposition of FCT or endorsed by Dr. Yurkovsky.

By now, it is readily apparent that the first book is an integral part of a new paradigm and testing methodology which I eventually named Intention Based Field Resonance Testing (IBFRT). The search for a suitable description of the power and legitimacy of basing a method of testing and treatment on subjective truth was underway. Soon this exciting work would be known by a new name. And, that name is whisperology.

SECOND BOOK

In the second book, *Intention Based Field Resonance Testing: The Power of the Whisper*, the anatomy and efficacy of the whisper are described. The power of the whisper is based on the interaction between intention and its target to create changes that benefit health on many different levels including the spiritual, mental, emotional, and physical planes. I described the emerging concepts and applications of whisperology as a response to being invited by the Divine to follow my own path:

The introduction of the word *whisperology* to express the power of intention in my work was, from my perspective, an example of what Dr. Bill Tiller meant when he wrote: "As we evolve to higher and higher states of consciousness it will be necessary for us to invent words to describe the new phenomena we are experiencing and the new perspective of the world that is unfolding within us. This initial language cannot be too precise and must contain room for ambiguity, like fuzzy logic or metaphors, because we have little experience with the new territory and the listener is likely to be at a different level in the consciousness band than ourselves."[47]

I wondered for some time, and consulted with Ardith, about including calibration numbers as a way of supporting the new findings, similar to how David Hawkins included calibration numbers in his books. In the end, I decided that Intention Based Field Resonance Testing and whisperology would need to stand on its own. If it would prove to be helpful to others then there was no need to include a number as a way to legitimize the truth of any of its principles. I wrote: "I wrestled with leaving the calibrations of any of his statements, or mine, in this book. I decided to omit them because I believe that the inclusion of a number does not really add to the substance of the book and may be an unhelpful, even polarizing distraction for some readers."[48]

In chapter 1, The Anatomy of a Whisper, I explained why I thought that the word *whisper* was well suited to capture the essence of my adventures with sending and receiving intention. I wrote: "I choose to use the term whispering instead of talking, shouting, preaching, explaining, or criticizing, because I want to play with certain ideas that suggest this to be a very special form of communication."[49] "I think the anatomy of a whisper includes the following elements: consciousness, intention, information, energy, and form… Incorporation of these five elements also places bioresonance testing, Including Field Control Therapy (FCT), into a larger context. I will be referring to this larger context, which defines my current clinical approaches, as Intention Based Field Resonance Testing… one might say there needs to be both a science and a spirituality about this business of whispering. To put it another way, we might suggest that the metaphor of whispering has a home above and

---

[47] Tiller, William A. *Science and Human Transformation* (Pavior Publishing, Walnut Creek, CA: 1997), p.297.
[48] Tonsager, *Intention Based Field Resonance Testing: The Power of the Whisper*, p. 41.
[49] Ibid, pp. 9-10

below the 499 thresholds, the threshold limit of science and reason, according to David Hawkins's Map of Consciousness."[50] "The Hawkins model is one of my favorite tools of choice for appreciating the physical, emotional, mental, and spiritual aspects of whispering."[51]

"Whispering captures the sense that we are connecting with others simultaneously on many different levels, from the most superficial and seemingly obvious ways to the deepest levels of our being. I believe that it is from within these deepest places, or realms, that we connect with one another, and where healing is to be found. If we consider the anatomy of a whisper, we realize that before any words are formed, there is intent to convey some information or purpose."[52]

An important aspect of whispering, the consciousness of the whisperer, was highlighted early and throughout the book. "This information is an expression of the intent of the whisperer. This information produces or manifests energies, qualities, and properties that are the multifaceted expressions of the level of consciousness of the whisperer."[53] "The power of the whisperer to communicate coherently with the whisperee increases when the whisperer increases his level of consciousness. This increase aligns the whisperer more closely with the fundamental universal consciousness of the Source."[54] "The seed crystal of any whisper is intention. Intention can build structures… When we use our intention from a high level of consciousness to build such structures, we are connected to a whole constellation of conditions and atmospheres that we could not possibly imagine from a previously smaller space

---

[50] Ibid.
[51] Ibid.
[52] Ibid.
[53] Ibid, p. 11
[54] Ibid, p. 17

(context)."[55] "For me, healing and whispering are closely related; they're possibly just two different ways of expressing the same stuff."[56]

In Chapter 2, Whispering Fundamentals, I responded to a question that many patients and practitioners asked me. "Can I whisper like you do?" My response to the question through a baseball analogy underscored what was required for Bill, Jean, and the rest of the meditators who were part of his imprinting team. For over fifty years, Bill and Jean practiced daily meditation—what he called "inner self-management methods." Bill wrote, "both Jean and I developed a sense of communion with, and subtle guidance from, consciousness in the 'unseen' domains of reality."[57] In my book, as I said in various ways to the people who asked me, "... there are no credentials, no training courses, no machines, or techniques, or magical gestures to make you into something essentially different than what you are."[58]

I am completely convinced that the contextual field of the whisperer is critical for effective use of my methods, because as I alluded to in Chapter 1, the consciousness of the whisperer is also being reflected, expressed, and manifested according to the five aspects of consciousness: intention, information, energy, activity, and form. The contextual field of the whisperer must be of sufficiently high coherence to create powerful intentions that can affect the consciousness of another person. Without a sufficient level of consciousness on the parts of both the whisperer and whisperee, the testing process is subject to error. If the consciousness of the whisperer is highly developed, it is possible to temporarily raise the consciousness of the whisperee through the intention of the whisperer, which creates a reliable testing situation."[59]

---

[55] Ibid, p. 18
[56] Ibid, p. 19
[57] Tiller, William A. *Psychoenergetic Science: A Second Copernican-Scale Revolution* (Pavior Publishing, Walnut Creek, CA: 2007) p. 16.
[58] Tonsager, *Intention Based Field Resonance Testing: The Power of the Whisper*, p. 22.
[59] Ibid, pp. 22-23

I concluded that the ability to whisper is limited if there is no daily spiritual practice. Without the faith and heart to be led in a new direction, to surrender the assumption of what we should find based on cherished beliefs or external authorities, we close the door to new discoveries and tactics."[60] "The relevance of the content of any findings is dependent upon both the mental software of the whisperer and divine grace and guidance."[61]

"I think that my drills describe a process for becoming an effective healer. The drills also reflect Dr. Tiller's list of necessary requirements, including a compassionate and loving heart, the development of a viable infrastructure needed for healing, the ability to broadcast or share this power, and the sharing of higher-dimensional energies with others."[62] One of my favorite expressions of Bill for engaging in this process is the following: "The procedure I followed on a daily basis was to both hold this general question and more detailed specific sub-questions of the day, like a brick in my open palms, during Jean's and my daily meditation—like a supplicant asking for guidance from the 'unseen'."[63]

Chapter 4 emphasizes that the power of the whisper is its connection to a fundamental level of consciousness with unlimited potential. The following excerpts from the chapter help the reader to appreciate the mystery and majesty of an integrous whisper. Here are a few samples:

"I believe that it is possible to expand our understanding beyond the limited world of materialism with faith, hope, love, the gift of grace, and the power of intention. This larger world is the realm of whisperology because it is an affirmation that consciousness is primary."[64]

---

[60] Ibid.
[61] Ibid.
[62] Ibid, p. 32
[63] Tiller, *Psychoenergetic Science: A Second Copernican-Scale Revolution*, p. 17.
[64] Tonsager, *Intention Based Field Resonance Testing: The Power of the Whisper*, p. 43.

"In the physical realm, we are invited to build models and pathways of causality, believing that we have captured all of the important facts. We use these facts to explain the causes of our troubles, our limited perception confuses necessary conditions as being causes. Dr. Hawkins states that 'the necessary conditions are spiritual qualities.'"[65]

"If consciousness is the primary source for the manifestation of our lives and health, we are mostly missing the mark in any approach that separates science from spirit."[66]

"I think that the term Source consciousness is sufficiently expansive to encompass my beliefs about the world of whisperology. Source consciousness is present in every level, every aspect of any system, from the simple to the most complex, from the smallest to the largest entities. A completely coherent entity is completely or fully conscious. *Whisperology* is the term that I currently use to express the idea that whispering increases the coherency of an entity by increasing its alignment with Source, with its own full consciousness, and with its purpose."[67]

"The anatomy of a whisper helps us to understand that the powerful potential in a whisper comes from the quality of consciousness of the whisper. Whispering tools interact with this enormous potential. The effects that are experienced by the whisperee demonstrate the power of kinetic energy; however, when we consider the five elements of a whisper, it might be more appropriate to say that kinetic information has expressed itself energetically, as evidenced by the energetic and physical changes in the whisperee. Why? Because a whisper at its most fundamental level is connected with a primary level of consciousness. This consciousness of the whisper and the intentions that express its consciousness exist as a potential. The intentions are actualized through information, energy, and structure. The structure is simply the end result.

---

[65] Ibid.
[66] Ibid, p. 45
[67] Ibid.

These ideas form the basis for explaining why whispering is such a powerful means of connecting with others."[68]

"Spiritual drills raise the consciousness of the spaces in which we live and work. Dr. Tiller refers to these as conditioned spaces."[69]

Chapter 5, Whispering Experiences, tells the story of a visit with a hypothetical patient named Helen. The interaction demonstrates the playful and compassionate interaction of a discovery process that must be individualized to bring healing. I offered the example in the form of a conversation because "my purpose for sharing my experiences through this format is to simply encourage you to think more about the mechanism and efficacy of whispering."[70]

One of the important aspects called mental incoherency was highlighted in the story about Helen. "Mental incoherency expresses the idea that the thoughts we hold are a powerful source of stress and obstacle to healing. These thoughts express the consciousness of the person who is thinking them and arise from the intentions of a particular level of consciousness. The particular information that is conveyed by these thoughts is the specifics, the 'facts,' used to describe what the person believes to be true. I cannot understand the words that Helen chooses to describe her current state of health without knowing the original context that has given birth to them! Her usage of the words comes from the specific qualities of Helen's consciousness."[71]

"No diagnosis or symptom is definitive. I use the different coherency measures to appreciate the individuality of every person I have the honor of seeing and testing. In my approach, every person is encouraged to become healthier, and the physical issues are seen as only a part (possibly the least important?) of the classroom called life."[72]

---

[68] Ibid.
[69] Ibid, p. 46
[70] Ibid. p. 47
[71] Ibid, p. 56
[72] Ibid, p. 70

Chapter 6, Intention Based Field Resonance Testing, explains why these words were chosen to describe the methodology of whisperology.

"I use the term *intention-based* to mean that love for the other person and the intention to help the person is integral to the testing. Most of the time, there is some conscious intention behind our activities. In intention-based testing, the entire process of testing is intended to be subjectively governed by the intentions of the tester. The goal is to test from a level of consciousness that is described as unconditional love."[73]

"This contrasts sharply with the idea that tests must be objective to have any value. The specific conscious intention that I am referring to is the state of being, or quality of consciousness, that crosses the 499 'bridge' in the Hawkins Map of Consciousness model. The inherent limitations of reason do not allow for a test that exceeds 499. To cross the 499 bridge, you need to follow a subjective path."[74] "The 499 bridge can be crossed because human beings contain the subtle energy structures to receive, build, and use it!... These structures are strengthened by positive intentions, thoughts, and emotions."[75] "The subtle energy network is strengthened by the letting go of limiting beliefs and negative emotions. It is strengthened through the practice of unconditional love."[76] "The power of intention changes lives."[77]

"As we continue to base our lives upon these intentions, we become more able through divine grace to let go of our grievances and all of our excuses for why others—and ourselves—should not be loved without disclaimers or exclusions. We eventually arrive at a place where the living of this intention has turned the key to awaken and build the structures and capacities that have been in us all along. We are also quietly certain that intending and acting from higher levels of consciousness act

---

[73] Ibid, p. 72
[74] Ibid, p. 73
[75] Ibid.
[76] Ibid, p. 74
[77] Ibid.

as a catalyst to awaken these qualities within others. This awakening is more akin to an encouraging whisper than a lecture or a procedure."[78]

"The word *field* is chosen here as a very expansive term that includes spiritual fields, consciousness fields, intention fields, mind fields, information fields, emotional fields, energy fields, and body fields... I think the word field is suggestive of a vast space or location that has a certain composition. The composition of the field will determine what entities, or types of consciousness, can grow and be sustained there. I am suggesting that the field is not a physical one, nor are the crops that are sown there necessarily visible in the fall produce section of your grocery store."[79]

"I choose the word *resonance* because it evokes a series of words in my mind including connection, attraction, communication, coherency, and recognition... I like to use the word resonance to describe the importance of these moments when changes take place... These moments can change the direction of your life and shift your attention to a different purpose... Resonance is recognized in a smile, a glimmer in the eye, a drop of rain at just the right place and time... It is magical. It is a purposeful connection... Resonance doesn't just happen as a random event. Perhaps resonance is generated through divine intention. I like to say thank God we're not in charge, for what does one person know about timing?... When resonance occurs, the moment is perfect for a whispering event."[80]

The word *testing* (instead of *therapy*, a word that is nearly owned by the medical field) is intended to suggest investigation into fields that are generally not considered to be significant regarding the improvement of health. The word is also intended to place the emphasis on the self-healing capacities within every person, a contrast to the idea that something 'therapeutic' is being done to another person. The testing is

---

[78] Ibid.
[79] Ibid, pp. 75-76
[80] Ibid, pp. 79-81

a discovery process that is intended to uncover information that the son being tested can use to become more conscious and coherent. whispering methodologies and the giving of informational remedies connect with the capacities that exist as an untapped potential in the person being tested. The testing leads to findings and strategies designed to restore or increase coherencies: physical, emotional, mental, and spiritual."[81]

The book included a Testing Procedure that brings together all of the elements that are relevant to IBFRT for discovery and imprinting. The book concludes with the same exhortation that each of us take on this journey of healing and discovery for the sake of others and ourselves: "Let each of us, in our wonderfully peculiar ways, follow our own divinely inspired path, and when they connect us with our brothers and sisters, let us laugh out loud with the knowledge that we on familiar territory with a family that is of more than direct biological origin. Let us never exchange our own uniquely personal paths for another because it would seem to make things easier, more expedient."[82]

With the conclusion of the second book, the world of whisperology was given the prominence which was anticipated within the first book. The basic concepts of whisperology and the rationale of IBFRT became the foundation for discovering how the power of intention could be magnified for more powerful and effective healing.

THIRD BOOK

In the third book, *Intention Based Field Resonance Testing: The Magnification of the Whisper*, the volume and accuracy of the whisper is explored.

In the introduction, The Evolution of Whisperology, I wrote: "I chose the term *whisperology* because it suggests an exploratory field of study beyond the conventional boundaries of science and medicine.

---

[81] Ibid, p. 82
[82] Ibid, p. 90

Whisperology is intended to encourage thoughtful yet playful concepts about and applications for the cultivation of intention in all aspects of our lives."[83] In keeping with the playful quality of whispering, I decided to change the format of the book. A series of conversations between myself and a person I called Morgan would be a means to demonstrate how understanding evolves through discovery and is facilitated by friendly and sometimes irreverent conversation between two friends.

In Chapter 1, The Whisperology Toolbox, I began to share findings with Morgan:

"I could not detect any difference between a human response to the numerical sequence and the remedy if the sequence of numbers was correct."[84]

"I learned how numbers could be used to objectify what the imaginal world was sharing with me through intention and alignment. This led to the creation of numerical scales for investigating levels of incoherency in many realms: spiritual, mental, emotional, physical, informational, energetic, and so on. Numbers helped me to bring these insights into a plane where I could see and explore the structure and meaning of coherency with its implications for human beings. This is an example of a consciousness-based and one could say also intention-based technology."[85]

In Chapter 2, The First Aspect of Magnification, a fundamental principle of whisperology, was introduced to Morgan. I encouraged Morgan to consider the limitations of human perception that does not believe in God. "The first aspect of magnification, therefore, is about the consciousness of the one who builds the toolbox, fashions its tools, and uses them."[86]

---

[83] Tonsager, *Intention Based Field Resonance Testing: The Magnification of the Whisper*, p. 1
[84] Ibid, p. 7
[85] Ibid, p. 8
[86] Ibid, p. 23

In Chapter 3, The Second Aspect of Magnification, Morgan is exposed to new ideas about the tools of whisperology. "The second aspect of magnification is about the creation and transformation of virtual structures using the tools of the whisperology toolbox."[87]

I said to Morgan, "So, in a virtual world, how do we see structures? We see them by objectifying the contents of the imagination… The appearances of these structures may be reminiscent of, or reflect known structures in the real world, however, because the imagination is the designer of the structures, these virtual structures might be completely different from familiar structures."[88]

I added, "With each structure, I build using the Hawkins scale and other scales that I developed for this purpose. Then I test it for its quality—that is, level of consciousness."[89] "I believe that the structures must come from devoted listening to the Source, the first aspect of magnification. Calibrating the structures of others and the principles used to build the structures is the work of the building inspector, who happens also to be me—yes, another way of defining subjective truth. To build more useful structures, I am required to follow my own path."[90]

"The inclusion of numbers in the technology of whisperology is intended to magnify the understanding, applicability, and efficacy of a whisper. I think that a numerical sequence is a means—but not the only means—to build or strengthen an informational structure, including that part of ourselves that could be regarded as an information structure. We might consider the informational structure to be an object, albeit a virtual one, that is built according to the instructions in the numerical sequence. The numerical sequence magnifies a whisper through specificity, through localization, to a well-defined target. The informational

---

[87] Ibid, p. 25
[88] Ibid.
[89] Ibid, p. 26
[90] Ibid, p. 29

structure creates, activates, and manifests an energy field by an unknown mechanism or process of manifestation."[91]

"Is there a virtual hearing or listening apparatus that understands these messages regardless of whether these messages come in numerical codes or not? I believe that such an apparatus exists... a virtual membrane that has an unknown relationship to the physical world, both symbolized and, in part, actualized at the cell membrane. This apparatus permeates or surrounds each membrane with a subtle structure that is not detectable by current testing methods."[92]

"Numbers both describe and define a target... Numbers also participate in what they describe, by creating influence and energy, giving direction, and ordering intention in a language that is universally known at the interface of every human cell—or perhaps in every space and domain of the universe...I see the interface as another way of expressing that every bit of our structure has its origins in unmanifested virtual information fields. The emergent nature of these fields is activated by intention. These fields are an aspect, or differentiation, of the ultimate information Source, the Creator, the Source of life, and the author of every code!"[93]

"The numbers are somehow a part of this fundamental quality of being or are able to express fundamental qualities of the Source's origin and expression, in each manifestation of being. Though the numbers look the same, I believe the form, substance, and manifestation of a number or a numerical array including a sequence operate according to different rules and have different behaviors and properties which are dependent on the level of consciousness."[94]

"At levels of consciousness beyond 499, the story of numbers is yet to be understood because it lies beyond the most sophisticated branches

---

[91] Ibid, p. 30
[92] Ibid.
[93] Ibid, p. 32
[94] Ibid, p. 33

of orthodox mathematics and physics. As such, it can only be described by the principles of a higher science, which come from a higher level of consciousness."[95]

In Chapter 4, Opening the Whisperology Toolbox, I address one of the most interesting topics uncovered thus far about the creation of numerical sequences:

Morgan poses the question, "If through your intention, your whispering, you are already creating informational medicines, what you call H vials and Source vials, then why bother with the numbers at all? Isn't that an extra and unnecessary step?"[96]

This is a valuable question and the main topic in this chapter. I respond, "…Because of the precision, because the language is known by others, whether they consciously understand it or not, the meaning is contained and expressed through the sequence. This makes a sequence available as a tool to share with others that can be accurately used by anybody… and that is true even if they don't or can't make their own whispering toolbox. They can still borrow your tools."[97]

"… It may be the case that someone else can't magnify a whisper as quickly or as powerfully as someone else, but there can't be any mistake that the correct tool was chosen for the target—they used a hammer when it was the best choice, and not a screwdriver or a wrench. The sequence ensures that the proper tool is used."[98]

"Intentions can be general or very specific. This affects the numerical sequences, including the number of digits needed to whisper the intention very accurately. The question is, what level of specificity is most helpful when it comes to sharing an intention?"[99]

---

[95] Ibid.
[96] Ibid, p. 34
[97] Ibid.
[98] Ibid, p. 35
[99] Ibid.

Morgan offers an apt description of why I write in the way that I do about whisperology. "You develop your analogies to find a way of expressing this form of communication because the conventional scientific language is barren and doesn't capture the human element, the subjective truth from which all the rest flows—including what everybody calls objective truth, the facts—right? But it's like you said… there is an objective truth for a particular level of consciousness; it is defined by the subjective truth for that level. But there is a different objective truth for a different audience that lives in a different world, in a different level of consciousness. You are trying to create a greater awareness about what you're doing than—…"[100]

In Chapter 5, Numerical Discrepancies, another interesting discussion takes place about the subjective nature of acquiring and using a numerical sequence. The existence of more than one sequence for presumably the same target raises interesting questions which are not lost on Morgan.

The explanation that I share with Morgan is both simple and multilayered. "The first reason for the difference between the numbers is the target."[101] "The numerical sequence is an example of specificity. A one is a one, not a two. So though the sequence is unequivocal, its target is not. The conscious and unconscious qualities of the person acquiring the sequence concerning a particular target—whether that be an ash tree or an oak tree—develop the sequence based on his specific intention."[102]

"I use my previously described methods to appreciate the specificity and inclusivity of numerical sequences by focusing intention upon different domains of a specific object. Developing sequences for different domains of the same object also reinforces the overall conception

---

[100] Ibid, p. 41
[101] Ibid, p. 44
[102] Ibid, p. 45

that to more fully comprehend any object, we must consider the object as a manifestation of its consciousness."[103]

"To develop the concept further, I focused intention upon the specific domains for a common object. This allowed me to appreciate that a sequence could be directed to one particular domain… sequences can be even more powerful when all domains are included in the development of a sequence."[104] "The sequences are different because the consciousness and intention that govern the use of the numerical sequence tool is primary. The consciousness and intention of the one developing the sequences accounts for the different sequences."[105]

"The development of sequences involves communication that is like a two-way street. This implies that we are not only sending out an inquiry, a whisper, but also listening to a very specific response to what has been silently uttered from within ourselves. Is it the response from another entity, or is it an echo?"[106]

"Numbers specify an intention in a way that words cannot. Numbers interact unconsciously with the human matrix to transform space, by delivering the intention without distortion."[107]

"I think the best numbers will be those that make us coherent on all levels, in all domains, in all aspects of our lives."[108]

In Chapter 6, Opening the Whispering Toolbox, I respond to Morgan's long expected request.

I said, Yes. "I will show you how the numbers are generated."[109]

"My hands are like instruments that listen to the responses that are returned to my whispers. I see with my hands; I hear with my hands; I

---

[103] Ibid, p. 46
[104] Ibid, p. 48
[105] Ibid, p. 49
[106] Ibid.
[107] Ibid.
[108] Ibid.
[109] Ibid, p. 51

whisper with my hands. Feeling satisfied with my answer yet? I didn't think so... My hands work together, but they have different functions. I do most of the whispering with my right hand and most of my listening with the left. The distance between the tip of the little finger and the thumb of my left hand is also a ruler, a scale, a graphing instrument. It sees the projected scale on the medial aspect of the right lower leg of the person I am testing... the responses to my whispers are sent there... the territory is mapped on your leg..."[110]

The answer was intended to be clear, but the reader may find it to be elusive and somewhat difficult to follow!

In Chapter 7, Adding More Tools to Another Drawer, Morgan's interests become more practical because he wonders how it is possible to know what to do when the information potential is unlimited. Morgan asks me, "With so many tissues, organs, cells, structures—how do you know where to begin? What would be most helpful?"[111]

I replied, "I don't know unless I consider incoherency. It is also why I don't diagnose anybody. I just listen—and I've become a very good listener. I whisper. I listen. I whisper back. When you listen first you know what is most important."[112]

Morgan asked for clarification. "...So, is that what you do then? You whisper to your patient, asking for an answer about what is most troublesome, most incoherent?"[113]

I brought the conversation back to coherence, a key word for IBFRT and powerful whispering. "The word troublesome is just fine, but I prefer the word incoherent. My asking includes not only something physical but also what may be emotionally, mentally, or spiritually incoherent."[114]

---

[110] Ibid, pp. 52-53
[111] Ibid, p. 56
[112] Ibid.
[113] Ibid, p. 57
[114] Ibid.

"Looking thoughtful, you said, "What you're telling me is that even though the sequences appear to be related to one another in a mathematical way, you believe it is a reflection of, or a translation of, a divine language that you do not understand but is somehow known unconsciously and universally at all levels, and in all domains, of creation."[115]

Morgan emphasizes a core belief that the numerical sequences are a whisper not an equation. "I understand better why you chose to think about these new developments as the magnification of the whisper—because you're talk about language, about communication, instead of a mathematical system."[116]

Chapter 8, The Drawer Within the Drawer, contains some hints of topics which will be central to the new book about fundamental structures and spaces. I shared with Morgan my quest to discover a level of organization that can be used to better understand the building blocks of informational objects. I said, "I thought that if there was a periodic table of elements—the one I learned several times and several levels of complexity—it was plausible to consider the possibility of fundamental—elemental—informational structures."[117] "To test the value of these informational sequences, I created an incoherency vial, and H vial, to identify primary information incoherence."[118]

I added, "Everything that is manifested in the universe has some type of consciousness."[119]

I decided that this was the appropriate time in the series of conversations to ensure that I continued to make a clear distinction between my use of numbers (as measures of incoherency as well as the numerical sequences) from David Hawkins' use of numbers (to calibrate the truth

---

[115] Ibid, p. 62
[116] Ibid, p. 63
[117] Ibid, p. 70
[118] Ibid, p. 71
[119] Ibid, p. 74

of a statement as well as the application of numbers to the Map of Consciousness). "The numerical sequence is to be distinguished from the Hawkins numbers of the Map of Consciousness that describe a level of consciousness. The maximum level for a physical structure of consciousness is 200. The maximum achievable level of consciousness ... to develop this consciousness is 499. This is the boundary of conventional science and a material paradigm. To cross the 499 threshold requires the involvement of domains of higher consciousness that are accessible through intention and the gifts of the Spirit that come from God..."[120]

"Through the powers of attention, attraction, and intention, IBFRT determines the level of consciousness and incoherency of the target. IBFRT identifies the conditions that interfere with or affect the manifestation of its target, by comparing the current state with its innate, original potential."[121] "Testing also determines what aspects may be addressed, by asking for God's blessing, permission, and guidance to pursue any incoherency..."[122] All decisions are intended to serve God, first, because the primary rule stated clearly in the first commandment may never be violated. This intent guides all testing. The second aspect is well known, and also silently confirmed; that the continued testing and treatment is to serve our neighbor. I believe this ensures as much as is humanly possible that any treatment, including the development of numerical sequences, is done with the closest alignment to the Source as possible. The precision of the alignment increases with the increasing consciousness and divinely guided intent of the one who is doing the testing. The ego is gently but firmly set aside."[123]

---

[120] Ibid, p. 83
[121] Ibid.
[122] Ibid.
[123] Ibid.

"I think you are getting the idea about what I do very clearly. The spiritual work opens the door to receive numerical sequences for whatever is required. Ask, and you shall receive. Numbers are received and sequences developed from a vast numerical sea... Numbers are pulled from God's ocean to normalize or restore what has been lost..."[124]

"After the numbers are imprinted into the other person, it is possible to describe the transformed state... I believe that the only way to prevent the whisper from being heard is to somehow have disingenuous intention... The final numerical sequences are very close but not 100 percent accurate depictions of the perfect, timeless, original, or eternal forms for each aspect of the target."[125]

In Chapter 9, Adding More Tools, the conversation returns to a more day to day subject. What may be done to help people that are dealing with the side effects of medications, including antibiotics and vaccines? I told Morgan, "Numerical sequences have proven to be very helpful to deal with the unwelcomed side effects of medications."[126] "The numerical sequences could be developed to apply to medications that were currently being taken, without interfering with the presumed benefits of the medication."[127] "I also confirmed that the elimination of the side effects for current medication lowers incoherency readings, including mental, emotional, and physical incoherency."[128] "In many instances, a single numerical sequence, typically a twelve-digit sequence, can be developed to eliminate the combined influence of all past medications. This eliminates the need to rely upon the patient's ability to recall all of the previous medication history."[129]

---

[124] Ibid, p. 84
[125] Ibid, pp. 84-85
[126] Ibid, p. 87
[127] Ibid, p. 88
[128] Ibid.
[129] Ibid.

The conversation was applied to Morgan's prescriptions which included several substances that are part of the prescription regimen of many people.

In Chapter 10, Opening the Whispering Toolbox, I tested and treated Morgan's friend. The treatment and conversation that follows provides the opportunity to demonstrate how the numerical sequences are an indispensable part of the whisperology toolbox. There is also an interesting exchange after the treatment in which Morgan asks me if I imprint any other content in the whisper besides numerical sequences. Here is what I said to him:

"Sometimes, I do whisper a series of statements. Let me give you an example. When the incoherent condition connected with vaccine incoherency was removed, my mind thought in this way: 'Let us remove the consciousness of all vaccine side effects from Allan's consciousness. From infinite past to infinite future, the consciousness of all vaccine side effects is removed from Allan's consciousness, never to return. Let us remove all of the informational structures of vaccine side effects from Allan's informational structures. From infinite past to infinite future, the informational structures of all vaccine side effects are removed from Allan's informational structures, never to return. Let us remove all of the energetic structures of vaccine side effects from Allan's energetic structures. From infinite past to infinite future, the energetic structures of all vaccine side effects are removed from Allan's energetic structures, never to return. Let us remove all of the physical structures of vaccine side effects from Allan's physical structures. From infinite past to infinite future, the physical structures of all vaccine side effects are removed from Allan's physical structures, never to return."

Morgan replied, 'And you do it in this way because your intent is to include all domains and all spaces, since time, too, is an element of space?'"

I answered, "Yes, and because what is most important to include is too small to see and too expansive to fathom."[130]

Chapter 11, The Structure of Whisperology, summarizes the whisperology model in two ways. First of all, Morgan offers his interpretation of what he understands from the conversations and his own personal experiences with the sequences (these are found in the book). Morgan does this in the form of a Journal Entry.

Morgan reads to me from his journal: "From the infinite resources of the soul, intention gathers and creates structures which have consciousness. These structures are manifested in a sequence, a kind of matrix. According to rules of assembly, organization, and behavior yet to be discovered which lie beyond the limits of reason or conventional science. These structures are the living containers that generate events. These events change the conditions of informational, energetic, and physical domains, in which time is a form of space. Changing these conditions increases coherence in all domains. And, most importantly, changes me."[131]

The second summary of the whisperology model is offered when I do a bit of artwork on the ground.

I drew a line about four feet long on the ground. Then I drew a second line that bisected the first perpendicularly, forming a cross. At the beginning of the first line, I placed a stone that was about the size of my fist. On the other end of the line, I placed a pebble. I took my reading glasses out of my pocket, placing them at the origin of the second line. On the other end of the second line, I placed the leaf. I placed a stick on top of the second line, connecting my glasses with the leaf.

"So there it is," I said. "You look really impressed. This is a representation of what I'm calling a four-element structure to represent manifestation. The big stone is the manifestation of the Source, a divine matrix of consciousness, intention, and information." Using another stick,

---

[130] Ibid, p. 107
[131] Ibid, p. 112

I drew a circle around the outside of the cross, with the circle's perimeter passing through the stone, the pebble, my glasses, and the leaf. "And this is the boundary."

Morgan asked, "I see the boundary and how you are connecting it with each element. What do you mean by boundary? The boundary of what?"

I said, "The boundary of the four-element structure is intended to represent the boundary of manifestation. Everything within the boundary is manifest in some domain, known or unknown. Outside the boundary, there are no limits. It is pure potential, without form or intent. Outside the circle, there is nothing to decide. It is the home of the Source. The boundary is created by an impulse from the Source. Everything inside the circle is a manifestation of the divine impulse. These four elements are the minimum requirements to create this structure. I call it the space of manifestation."

Morgan quickly added, "So, I'm guessing that if the big stone is the manifestation of Source, of God, then the pebble is a person, a soul, a human matrix of consciousness, intention, information, energy, physical structure… a chip of the old block, a piece of rock from a mountain of granite…"

"Yes, that's what I mean. You're starting to sound a bit like me with your metaphors. That's a little scary. Anyway, that brings us to the other axis. My glasses are meant to represent my intention, my consciousness, how I perceive my world, I replied."

Morgan asked, "And, what about the leaf?"

I answered, "This is the object, the target, of my intentions, my inclination, my tendency to always be perceiving something… my understanding of what the leaf is, and the rest of the world that I consider to be reality."

Choosing his words carefully, Morgan offered these words. "Yes, I remember the day when we talked about the ash tree in your front yard, you said thoughtfully, your glasses are a symbol of your intentions, your perception, the lens through which you see and experience the world. Everything inside the circle is connected to everything else inside the circle, isn't it?"

I confirmed that he understood what I was trying to convey to him through the diagram. "That is my perception, my belief. When consciousness expands, the connections between the small stone and the rock become more obvious. The axis between them has always been there, but through my glasses, I see them move close together, maybe so close together that the pebble fuses with the stone. When consciousness expands and one moves in the direction of the land of 600—"

Excitedly, Morgan interrupted, "Then the axis between your glasses and the leaf is shortened. Maybe it becomes so short that you become the leaf. Your glasses disappear inside the leaf because the duality is gone. Everything has merged in the middle of your circle into an infinitely small point; the stone, the pebble, the glasses, the leaf, everything."

I can only smile when I think about the conversation when I say, "Yes, something along those lines. We could have said it the other way, too, that everything expands into a circle of infinite size. It really amounts to the same thing, just a different way to express oneness. I think each element is an essential part of my whispering. The sequences help me to bring the elements together, closer to one another, somehow. Beside the two axes, we could also draw lines that connect the four elements together, around the perimeter, to create a square inside the circle. I used my stick to inscribe the lines to show you what I meant."

And later in their conversation, Morgan adds one more comment that recognizes his understanding of what has taken place between them during their dinners and other adventures. "I see what you mean. The axis between the stone and the pebble is the first aspect of magnification— 'My soul doth magnify the Lord." The axis between the eyeglasses and the leaf is the second aspect of magnification. When consciousness is increased, everything moves in the direction of unity. It gets infinitely small, or big—you're right, it really is the same thing..."[132]

As I mentioned earlier, I think this form of sharing the new developments was an excellent tool for making a subject that could easily be too abstract or ethereal, an entertaining book. The feedback from patients and practitioners to the third book has been especially positive. When I finished the book, it was completed with the awareness of one more book, a final book, to further explore what I drew on the ground for Morgan. The evolutionary nature of whisperology is reflected in the conclusion of this book. I wrote:

"The whispering continues. The sequences continue to appear from the inside of a circle that cannot be described, visualized, or constructed according to the rules of geometry. I doubt there will be an end to the sequences I receive. I think it is unlikely that I will ever be left with a final sequence to whisper, a last group of numbers, when I will say that the whispering is all done and there are no more things to whisper. I think the world of whisperology is just getting started."[133]

I hope that these comments about the previous books will help all of you to understand how the geometry of the whisper adds to the theory and application of whisperology. Now it is time to get to it and introduce the new tool!

---

[132] Ibid, pp. 113-116
[133] Ibid, p. 118

PART I. THE NEW TOOL

CHAPTER ONE
Introducing the new tool

The new "tool' in the whisperology toolbox is an isosceles triangle which is composed of 63 smaller isosceles triangles. I will always refer to this particular triangular structure as The Figure, which is included with other diagrams at the end of the book.

I expect that your initial response to the introduction of the new tool, and its application in whisperology, might include these two questions:

The first question: Why did you choose an isosceles triangle and not some other shape?

The second question: What do triangles have to do with consciousness, science, or healing?

I will do my best to answer these questions.

The First Question
Why did you choose an isosceles triangle and not some other shape?

I did not choose the isosceles triangle, or decide how it is partitioned into 63 smaller triangles. *The triangle chose me. Yes, I do really mean to answer you in this way.* I hope this answer captures your attention. Perhaps you object, "What do you mean, the triangle *chose* you? Triangles do not choose anything!"

The triangular structure was not developed through a logical process. Nor did I kidnap the structure from an obscure book about sacred geometry. I believe the isosceles triangle structure —The Figure—was "given" to me when I evolved to a level of consciousness that the new tool could be used to expand whisperology. For most people, I expect that is a "no answer" answer. I believe that the "choosing" or "being chosen" is not personal at all. That is not what I mean! I think a more accurate explanation is to suggest that when intention is focused upon a particular task, and intention is functioning within a particular field of consciousness, then the information, or "answers," that become available *reflect the impersonal qualities of that level of consciousness.*

Access to these higher fields is a consequence of spiritual work. Hawkins writes, "Spiritual work, therefore, is primarily a letting go of the presumably known for the unknown, with the promise of others who have done it that the effort is more than well rewarded at the end. On the earthly level, gold is not created but merely revealed by chipping away that which obscures it. One of the main spiritual tools is intention which sets up priorities and hierarchies of values that energize one's efforts. Spiritual work is a commitment and also an exploration. The way has been opened by those who have gone before and set the possibility in consciousness for others to follow."[134]

I will try to explain the process that was taking place within me when I began to work with the potential appearance of the new tool.

---

[134] Hawkins, David R. *The Eye of the I* (Veritas Publishing, Sedona, Arizona: 2001) p. 117.

Before the first triangular structures were created, I was busy with projects using numerical sequences. I created so many numerical sequences of varying numbers of digits, and for many purposes, I wondered if it would be possible, or even helpful, to create a manual of sequences, as I alluded to in the third book. Many sequences had a general application that could be used by any person because the sequence described a particular substance, like histamine, for example, or a structure, like the bursa of the shoulder. Any person experiencing stress from elevated histamine benefits by using a sequence to balance histamine; or, in the case of bursitis of the shoulder, a sequence to create coherency in the bursa of the shoulder. However, many sequences were specific to an individual health concern. For example, a person experiencing pain from a past injury benefitted from a sequence that is unique to the circumstance of the injury. It did not seem very useful to create a manual with a thousand different sequences for injury.

There was a second consideration while I worked on the development of a manual: Simplicity. I wanted to find a way to create a system that any person could use with no medical or scientific background required. This encouraged me to think about the sequences from a different perspective. One of the outcomes of the search for a fundamental and easily used series of numbers was the identification of numerical sequences for every element of the periodic table.

Every person would benefit by a sequence to balance calcium, selenium, iron, or any other element that was essential to human health. I developed sequences for every element and discovered that imprinting elemental sequences produced beneficial effects. This led to further investigation of novel ways to organize the elements, besides the periodic table, that were not based on the atomic numbers. Could the elements be organized in a non-linear structure that expressed a higher level of coherency and larger context than their physical properties? These efforts also reinforced an emerging belief, that *the elements, as well as the sequences, are conscious, and in some way, living entities* but the answer to how or why this might be beneficial is beyond my pay grade, my current level of consciousness.

The creation of the elemental sequences expanded my inquiries in new and unexpected directions! *I became more aware that what is understood about the elements as objective facts reflects the limited but very useful positionality of science* which reaches its highest capacity to understand at 499 on the Hawkins Scale of Consciousness. To believe that the element is fully known at the 499 level only reflects the bias of science *and its limiting beliefs*. I discovered that each element also is governed by spiritual laws from the non-linear domain beyond the physical world. Morgan and I discussed these possibilities in our second to last meeting when I helped his friend Allan.[135]

I realized through IBFRT that there were more fundamental elements than atoms like carbon or oxygen. What were these elements? How many were there? Were the elements of the same variety as the subatomic particles of physics, or, something completely different? What is the relationship between these more fundamental elements and the current periodic table? Could I locate their manifestation within The Figure? Will these fundamental elements be found in human beings and/or somewhere else? What is their connection to human health? I was moved to keep asking, keep whispering, keep listening... So many questions and not nearly enough answers.

The daily drills helped me to live with the questions until it was time for a new answer, a larger context from which to provide the previous content and context of whisperology with a deeper meaning. This is not the reward for doing "the drills," like you are performing the task of a martyr or ascetic, and you should get something for your hard "work," but rather the experience of divine grace that uses the drills and

---

[135] Tonsager, *Intention Based Field Resonance Testing: The Magnification of the Whisper*, p. 108.

the power of intention to transcend the perception of opposition or obstacle. In my own way, I am engaged in a similar process that assisted Dr. Tiller to use his meditative practices as a means to find answers to profound questions in a conceptual framework that exceeded the constructs of conventional science.[136] When new insights appear, I believe that it is the evolution of consciousness through divine grace, that expands awareness to a greater level of clarity that has always been available but remained hidden until the appropriate moment. *Awareness is expanded by letting go of what we think we know so that we might see reality in a new way, from a more evolved positionality than the upper limits of science.*

I am not always sure there is a place in this world for anyone to be taken seriously if he or she uses the word *revelation*, but that is what I would call the process that was taking place during these investigations. The word *inspiration* is more palatable—Edison-like. Inspiration is not a bad word but I think it suggests too much credit be given to the one who expresses the inspiration because all revelation is divinely inspired and *impersonal. A gift.* If you accept the notion of a God that is not only transcendent but imminent then perhaps it is best to say that I have learned to attune more easily and closely to an Inner Voice, or Field, a whisper that in some way originates from the Great Unseen. The voice is like a Teacher who provides spiritual guidance and vision that appears to be independent from what I know, or think I know. This Inner Voice led me to the following level of understanding about the new tool and provides potential answers in accordance with the limitations of my own vision and context.

I imagine that some readers might describe this form of inspiration as a silly and unscientific exercise in imagination or creative thinking. There might be a different group of readers who might speak about The Figure as an archetype, the activation of a timeless form from what Carl Jung called the collective unconscious. For me, I would state it more

---

[136] Tiller, *Psychoenergetic Science: A Second Copernican-Scale Revolution*, p. 17.

simply: The Figure was an answer to prayer, a gift from God that, with humble intention, may be used for spiritual growth and discernment. As I mentioned previously, I am quite certain that the theories and applications of The Figure may easily be dismissed by the scientific community as foolish and a waste of time, or by the religious community as heretical, or worse.

However, for me, I realized that The Figure was a means to organize a qualitatively different table of elements than the familiar periodic table of elements. I regard The Figure as a map of spiritual elements, or, spiritual *spaces*. This level of understanding was, and is, what has been whispered to me!

The Second Question

Your second question: What do triangles have to do with consciousness, science, or healing?

The answer to the second question is powerfully connected to a quality of life that I describe by using the word *coherence*. The Figure is used to locate triangles which *represent* contextual spaces in which there are physical and non-physical incoherencies. The content, or specific nature of the incoherence, is *symbolized* by the area within the triangle. IBFRT uses The Figure to locate which triangle is the most helpful element, or *space*, to address a particular "problem." If there is a problem, then, the space inside the triangle is not coherent. The degree to which the space is not coherent is determined by IBFRT. Once the connection within the consciousness of the whisperer (the one who is performing IBFRT) has been established between the problem that is being experienced by the patient, and the triangle that contains, or manifests, the incoherence, a numerical sequence is created by IBFRT that will carry and magnify the whisper. Through the imprinting process, in the form of a powerful whisper, the space within the triangle becomes more coherent. Not only does the particular triangle that was the target of the whisper become more coherent, other *related triangles* become more coherent. I interpret the findings with the related triangles as evidence of an expansion of context in which healing takes place simultaneously within several domains, physical and spiritual.

The Figure is a tool created by, and used by, consciousness, for healing. With the assistance of The Figure to locate the source of the incoherent conditions, physical or spiritual, the whisperology toolbox has added *a contextual tool*. What does this mean? Each triangle of The Figure symbolizes a particular context and its connection to a different aspect of consciousness. For example, some triangles are connected to the *consciousness* of an organ or tissue. Other triangles are connected with a spiritual element, or space, that reflects emotional, mental, karmic, or spiritual coherence. (The different qualities of the 63 triangles will be a topic of discussion in a subsequent chapter.)

For the present moment, the essential point to keep in mind is the following: when IBFRT leads to the identification of a particular space, that is, a particular triangle, we are provided with additional information about the context of the "problem." For example, a problem that was believed to be a physical problem is shown through The Figure to be, at its core, an emotional problem, or the manifestation of a spiritual struggle. The case studies that will follow are intended to demonstrate how The Figure is used to identify the essential problem, which may be very different than how it has been perceived by the patient or conventional medicine.

In a larger frame of reference, a new conceptual network that includes but transcends conventional science, healing occurs in consciousness through the removal of incoherent conditions. *Healing occurs when the context of the one who experiences suffering is changed.*

A Unified Theory

The advent of a new tool is accompanied by the anticipation of putting it to good use. Unlike the many tools that are used to build a home,

The Figure did not come in a tool case with a parts list and set of directions to use it safely and wisely. Using a sledgehammer to hammer a finishing nail will not only bury the nail into a piece of trim but damage the wood. Using a Sawzall, a reciprocating saw, to cut quarter round trim will do more than cut the trim because it is used for demolition, not finishing work. Knowing which tool is the best one to use for a particular task not only requires instructions for its usage but an overall understanding of how each task only makes sense within the larger framework of the design of the house.

There is a shared level of consciousness among most people living in the "modern world," that an obvious difference exists between what is required to build a solid foundation for a home, and what options are available to give a room the finishing touch. The composition and design of every tool is intended for a specific purpose that makes sense within a general purpose. While there are differences between houses, there is general agreement about what needs to be done, and in what order. The abstraction of the general purpose of the house including its composition and design is the blueprint. The raw materials and tools used by skilled workers manifest the intention of the architect. Every part of the construction of the home begins in the consciousness of the designer. One might even say that the architect is in every brick and nail.

Like the blueprint of a home that includes every specification of its design and the materials to be used for its construction, wouldn't it be perfect if we were in possession of such a plan that was as simple to read for the design and construction of a human being? When a home is damaged by a storm, or falls into disrepair through neglect, there are well known and agreed upon solutions to make the repairs, or do the remodeling. The theories and practices of home construction are sufficient to respond to almost any situation. Wouldn't it be amazing to be able to have access to the tools and raw materials to do the same with human beings? The conventional world of science and technology seems to believe that it is only a matter of time before the full plans behind the construction of a human being are elucidated. If a new part is needed then all that will be required is a 3D printer to replace it.

A *physically-based* unified human Theory of Everything (TOE), appeals to the level of consciousness that is unable to cross the 499 bridge. The greatness of the achievements of science conceals the smallness and impoverishment of its conception of the human being because the positionality from which it proclaims success is severely limited. Every TOE about human beings, no matter how many parts are required to assemble the human house, is completely dependent on its context, the consciousness of the TOE "holder." *Transcend the context and the previous TOE turns out to be only a toenail.*

The Figure depicts other aspects of Human than a physically based blueprint because it is a *spiritual illustration*. The essential quality of Human will not be found within the detailed descriptions in the physical sciences of anatomy, physiology, or biochemistry because the context is too limited. In what textbook would you find the picture or biochemical pathway that explains what it means to be made in the image and likeness of the Creator? How does one comprehend the divine intention expressed in Genesis, or other spiritual traditions?

The words in Genesis are a complete yet not fully comprehended human TOE because so much of what unfolds in the human experience is left for us to explore through our own spiritual development. Working with The Figure enables its user to explore the *spiritual anatomy* of Human. The intention is to unify the observations and experiences with The Figure into a single, complete theory, a TOE, that does not exclude but transcends the theories of a physically based conventional model. Bill Tiller calls this an expanded frame of reference that includes what is considered to be the "subjectively" human such as thoughts, feelings, intention, and consciousness which have no place in the "objective" model of conventional science.

The design and composition of The Figure encourages those who use its triangles to adopt an expanded frame of reference which invites exploration of the ultimate TOE. That is, what does it mean to be made in the image and likeness of the Creator? An exhaustive and satisfying conception of the human being may never be attainable; however, The Figure expands the context and application of whisperology by not only including but giving primacy to matters of the soul over biology. Obviously, the desire to fully describe the spiritual anatomy of Human with a new unified theory is subject to the significant limitations of this particular TOE "holder" and the realization that any new spiritual TOE, however, wonderful or useful, including The Figure, is also a mere toenail, a helpful abstraction, but far from complete.

CHAPTER TWO
Tool Design and Composition

The Figure is a *spatial* tool because the constellation of triangles functions as a map to guide its user, *the whisperer*, to the correct triangle to send or receive a whisper. Consciousness may be compared to a global positioning system (GPS) which furnishes the guidance to determine positionality and destination within The Figure. The governing geometry of the whisper, with its overall triangular structure, and 63 triangular elements, establishes a virtual map that may be used by consciousness to explore the terrain of the soul.

The Figure assists its user with finding specific information in what is commonly referred to as The Field, a vast virtual network that holds every bit of information about the universe. The tool is used to find the relevant information to recontextualize a particular "problem" and develop the intention to solve it. Every intention and target of whisperology is connected with a certain triangle on the map. The target may be an organ like the liver, a cell like an osteocyte, a health problem like coronary artery disease, a past accident like a concussion, or an emotionally traumatic situation. The map is applicable to contexts of any size or scale whether it be atoms, cells, human beings, or planets.

Incoherencies of any type are experienced as problems that come in every imaginable shape and size. Limited perception about the true nature of the human condition is expanded when there is awareness of the essential connections between physical, emotional, mental, karmic, and spiritual incoherencies. The Figure is of invaluable assistance when the relevance of *all forms of incoherence* are included to identify a new positionality about a familiar problem. Regardless of the type of incoherence, or when the incoherence occurred, or will occur in the future, the tool is used to locate the space in which it exists, or through which it will express its potential. Identifying the location of the incoherency within a particular triangular space enhances the ability of the whisperer to hear and send a whisper.

I will try to explain how this method is used with several examples in the second part of the book, but as I discovered with Bill, this will be a great challenge.

Tool Design

I mentioned earlier that I was given The Figure as a gift from an Inner Teacher. This tool was shared with me through a series of steps about its design and composition in which a primary question was answered followed by a "homework" assignment, which included playing with triangles like a child in kindergarten. Making the triangles was fun and sometimes exhilarating.

Then, there would be another question, and with the answer to the question, yes, of course, you guessed it, more homework. Sometimes, the response to the homework was a simple and clear "No—not acceptable." I understood this to mean that my efforts did not meet the standards of the Teacher because I was capable of doing a better job with my assignments. This experience of an incomplete, or only partially accurate understanding of the answer to a question, occurred more than once! During this creative period, I surrendered most, if not all, of what I thought I knew about chemistry, or the periodic table. I simply played.

I hoped that when I got it right, the inner Teacher would let me know. Many structures were created before class came to an end. The final assignment for this class was given a passing grade when The Figure was completed.

The Figure depicted 63 related spaces. In every triangle, the vertex angle is 25.2 degrees and the base angles 77.4 degrees. I smiled when I realized that 2 + 5 + 2 = 9 (the sum of the digits of the vertex angle) and the base angle is 7 + 7 + 4 = 18 = 1 + 8 = 9 (the sum of the base angle). The sum of the internal angles of a triangle is always 360 degrees which is also 3 + 6 + 0 = 9. *And, obviously, 63 triangles = 6 + 3 = 9.*

All of the triangles in The Figure are similar, that is, they are isosceles triangles that share common angles. Within the seven groups, each of the nine triangles which constitute one of the seven major triangles are not only similar, they are also congruent, meaning they not only have the same angles but the lengths of the sides are also the same. In some of the seven groups, six of the triangles point upward and three triangles point downward. In some of the groups it is exactly the opposite because six of the triangles point downward and three triangles point upward. Intriguing! Groups one, five, and six are the largest triangles and are similar and congruent with each other. Groups two, three, four, and five are the smallest triangles and are similar and congruent with each other. The combined areas of groups two, three, four, five are equal to the area of group one, five, or six. Groups two, three, four and five are similar but not congruent with groups two, three, and five. All of the triangles within groups two, three, four and five are similar but also congruent with each other. All of the triangles within groups one, five, and six are similar but also congruent with each other. (See Figure 1. "The Figure," Figure 2. "The Seven Primary Triangles," and Figure 3. "The Nine Triangles In A Primary Triangle" in the Appendix)

I believe there is a rich world of inner meanings that remains to be explored based on the coherence and beauty of the triangular patterns.

Each triangle has its own qualities but remains connected and communicative with the others. This is symbolically represented by the lines and vertices they share in common. The Figure bears some resemblance to other geometrical figures that have been significant to others throughout the history of sacred geometry, but I realized that my task was defined by an awareness that The Figure would become a new tool in whisperology. Everything that is described in this book is in some way related to the central role of The Figure.

Yes, I was having fun and not feeling too silly about it because I knew something about the efforts of modern and ancient man to investigate the properties of shapes and numbers from a spiritual perspective. As I have written previously, numbers are for more than counting! I wondered about the significance of this highly coherent structure that somehow reflected the 63 (6 + 3 = 9) spiritual elements that had a different organization than the well-known figures of sacred geometry. Ultimately, it didn't matter. I needed to focus my attention on the triangle that chose me!

There are times when I look at The Figure, or trace its lines with my fingers, that I experience what I will call a *resonance*—a kind of inner "knowing-ness" that The Figure reflects, a deep wisdom about a unifying primary structure in the non-linear domain that is common to all human beings and human experience—and perhaps beyond that! I intend to explore—to the upper limit of the context in which I reside—what The Figure is expressing about the context of human life and the evolution of human experience in the classroom called daily life. These resonant moments are hard to describe because the experiences are subjective not objective. You can't stand in someone else's shoes—you have to learn to find and fill your own footwear.

Tool Composition
Eventually, I realized and confirmed through the testing that the 63 elements are organized into seven groups with nine elements in each

group. This *hierarchy of space* is evident in The Figure. I suppose it might be called a virtual, or, spiritual periodic table of elements, forces, or spaces. Just as there are different criteria into which the elements of the periodic table are organized (properties, atomic number, valence, etc.), there appear to be several ways to appreciate the relationships between the seven primary triangles, a subject which will be introduced in a later chapter.

The completion of more homework assignments led to the understanding that there was a hierarchical structure of the spaces that bore some relationship to the organization of human physical structures, as well as spiritual values, and the human experience, or perception, of temporal events. The structural organization was calibrated for its correspondence with the Eastern theories that describe human beings through a series of subtle bodies and chakras. The correlation between The Figure and the Eastern model is about 93 percent. The appendix includes a diagram (See Figure 4. "Correlation Between The Figure and Seven Chakras) which depicts the relationship between The Figure and the chakra system. Interesting.

Most importantly, if it has not already dawned on you, the power of The Figure is not that it exists out there, somewhere, but exists *within us*, in every level of organization. Like the architect who is connected to every nail and shingle in a blueprint for a home, the design and composition of the tool reflects the image and likeness of the Creator, the Great Unseen. The Figure is a primary expression of the physical and non-physical aspects of our being.

A New Antenna

The design and composition of the tool is to accomplish its intended purpose! That is obvious but what exactly is the purpose of The Figure? There are a number of ways to speak about this purpose and I hope at least one of the conceptualizations will make sense to the reader.

One helpful conceptualization is to regard The Figure as an antenna that both receives and broadcasts intention, which is communicated in many forms—including numerical sequences. The Figure is like an antenna, used by consciousness through the power of intention and divine grace, to expand "bandwidth" to become conscious of more information, a larger contextual field, in order to receive and send whispers from any location. In electronics, an antenna that both sends and receives information is called a reciprocal antenna.

The 63 antennas work in concert with one another as a unified network of "spiritual antennas" which send and receive spiritual information. Like an antenna, each triangle is tuned to one of the 63 spiritual elements which influence a particular meridian, chakra, subtle energy network, part of the body, earth, universe, level of reality.... Each triangle is sending and receiving intention from within a spiritual realm, a spiritual center.

Analogous to any antenna, which is designed to optimize certain properties like sensitivity to a particular frequency range, maximum bandwidth, or optimal signal to noise ratio, The Figure is designed to perfectly accomplish its purpose. Like any antenna, the size and shape of the 63 connected triangles is a function of the purpose of The Figure. Therefore, the consciousness of The Figure, itself, is expressed in the particular shape of the isosceles triangle, the particular internal angles, and the perfectly arranged network of 63 interconnected triangles. The shape and structure of the spiritual spaces of The Figure enhances the transmission and reception of intention, information, energy, and healing.

The numerical sequence creates and carries intention through a virtual non-linear pathway in order to manifest and magnify the whisper for maximal transmission and reception. The geometry of The Figure reflects a fundamental common dimensionality between the governing presence and creation, *including Human*.

It is worth repeating that *there could be no whispering without humans being equipped with the same reciprocal antennas.* The common dimensionality is known by a familiar phrase to most people: the human is fashioned in the image and likeness of its Creator. The intrinsic dimensionality within Human reflects its spiritual origin and is expressed in every level of being.

The relationships between the networks of the seven primary triangles also symbolizes another essential aspect about the coexistence of the physical and non-physical nature of Human. Dr. Tiller's working hypothesis is that matter exists within consciousness. Consciousness is an emergent property of the interaction between spirit and matter within the physical realm. "Antenna-like" connections include both body and spirit.

The analogy of reciprocity between a divine and human antenna is useful because it is a means of helping consciousness to clarify how coherent communication between the two "antennas" raises consciousness and reduces all forms of incoherence.

The power source for the antenna is intention. The analogy of the reciprocal antennas guides the human to identify an optimal location within The Figure, meaning which particular triangle—which particular governing presence—is the most helpful to improve the quality of tuning through a conscious, intentional alignment. For example, there appears to be a problem with the operation of the right shoulder. The inner question that is whispered might be constructed as follows: to which space, to which governing presence, to which antenna, does my right shoulder need to be coherently tuned to in order for my right shoulder to be healed, to function according to its unique and sacred purpose? There is a particular triangle for a particular alignment, a sacred antenna that may be fully tuned to the particular antenna for the aspect of the right shoulder that is the object of attention. A similar approach is applicable to non-physical obstacles. There will be triangles in which immobilizing fear, depression, or apathy is located.

The reciprocal relationship between Human and its Creator is present within every aspect of human existence, physical or non-physical. Whispering the request to identify the antenna location within The Figure is easily done by looking at The Figure, or holding a mental image of The Figure in mind, to hear the answer. Once the answer is received, the receiver may use the tools of whisperology to strengthen and magnify the connection between the two "antennas" through prayer, meditation, or the development of a numerical sequence. Imprinting the intention creates a high level of coherence between the two antennas, a resonant state (a grace filled moment) in which healing takes place.

Where does the tool come from?

Everyone who purchases a tool need only check the box, or the tool itself, to know who manufactured the tool and when and where it was built. Consumers frequently compare brands when they are trying to find the best tool. So, you ask, just where does this tool come from? Who makes it? How reliable is it to do what it is supposed to do?

These are reasonable questions, appropriate follow up questions to the first two questions from Chapter 1. My answer to these questions is simple but not necessarily easy to understand or believe. I am fond of saying, "I can live with that."

Where does the tool come from? The tool which I refer to as The Figure comes from another realm of meaningful primary reality that transcends time and space.

Who makes the tool? Consciousness creates the tools of numbers, words, symbols, and patterns, like The Figure.

How reliable is The Figure to do what it is supposed to do? Because The Figure is a *subjective* tool, the efficacy and accuracy of its application will always depend on its user. When the tool is used by an integrous person, The Figure is a means of realizing Self. When the tool is used with humble intention for spiritual growth and discernment, The Figure is a vehicle of healing and transformation.

Consciousness must rely upon itself. Consciousness uses these tools to construct and interpret itself, and what it has created including concrete reality. All of the tools of whisperology are created in a realm of consciousness that also includes the tool of The Figure. *This is the process by which consciousness may discover itself.* The Figure is a self-portrait of the essence, potential, and power of human coherence. The Figure is a symbol of its timeless presence in all that exists.

The Figure is a tool which connects the human experience, perceived in space time as a series of linear events, with the non-linear realm of consciousness in which all creative potential originates. Creation is the Unmanifest becoming Manifest within the universe including Human. The Figure is a simple,—*a wonderfully simple*—picture of a spiritual design, an invisible blueprint which exists within every level of organization and complexity.

The description of The Figure that is most comprehensive is to simply view it as an abstraction of the process through which the Unmanifest becomes Manifest. This description is the most coherent and accepted IBFRT finding because the abstraction is not restricted to Human, or a particular quality or aspect of Human. The work with The Figure demonstrates the applicability to human experience but extends awareness of the full potential of Human to include universal coherence and connection beyond any definition of an essential separation between Human and Universe, between soul and cosmos. This understanding is expressed in a portion of the daily meditation. "For in the brilliance of the Light, our spiritual vision is restored, and we honor the one Light that stands behind and beyond, permeating every appearance including our own."[137]

Universal coherence includes, in the human TOE, the mind-boggling assertion that *the entire universe is also in the bio-body suit*. The statement implies an awareness that I will refer to as "entity coherence."

---

[137] Tonsager, *Intention Based Field Resonance Testing: The Magnification of the Whisper*, p. 126.

These entities include local (earth-centric) and universal entities. Local entities include microscopic beings, like bacteria and other microorganisms, as well as plants and every species of life on earth, from salmon to salamanders to Shetland ponies. Local coherence also includes what is often deemed lifeless or inert, such as rocks or soil, air and water. Universal coherence includes everything beyond our local planet that is mostly foreign and unknown to humans. The local and universal entities influence the consciousness of Human in the physical, karmic, and spiritual domains.

The Figure is used to explore all forms of coherence within consciousness that challenge beliefs about what it means to be human, especially the cherished notion that every person is fundamentally different and separate from another. The misperception of separation, and its attachment to the fear of survival, is a fundamental component of the operating software of nearly every human being. Limiting beliefs based on separate and "personal" identities explains why there is little evidence in the words and actions of most people that would suggest that we are essentially one. In truth, *nothing is personal.*

In short, there seems little that the new tool cannot do!

CHAPTER THREE
Contextual Space and Coherence

Contextual Space

The triangle is the most simple and perfect symbol of a contextual space. The space creates separation. Simply and elegantly, an inside and an outside comes into being. There is a boundary established when potential is created. In two dimensions, the smallest geometrical figure that can enclose space, and separate this space from the rest of space, is a triangle. I stay with two dimensions, following the Inner Teacher, because The Figure symbolizes the fundamental difference between inclusion and exclusion, subject and object, linear and nonlinear, material and spiritual, potential and realization, appearance and essence, form and formlessness.

There is an inside and an outside defined by three lines of infinite thinness that could not be more precise. No zone of any size exists between the inside and outside of the triangle like a neutral or demilitarized zone between warring countries. The design and composition of the tool allows its user to distinguish one contextual space from another. One is either inside or outside of the triangle. There is no middle ground, no "sitting on the fence."

I playfully remind the reader, once again, that the triangle, and network of triangles, "chose" me. With the completion of these assignments, my attention turned to the task of identifying the most coherent way of interacting with its spaces—yes, through whisperology. *Different spaces in The Figure symbolize different contexts of human experiencing.*

Let us consider each triangle of The Figure as a container of space, a *contextual space*. I define contextual space to mean a space that is characterized by a group of rules which govern the properties inside the space, including the content of that which may be found within its perimeter. The 63 spaces must share common rules, or governing principles, because each triangle is part of the entire space, however, there are also specific rules, or specific governing principles that distinguish one contextual space from another. We will explore what these rules might encompass when we compare the interaction of IBFRT with the seven primary triangles.

I propose that there are 63 unique but intrinsically connected contextual spaces, which define 63 different ways of manifesting potential into time space. Moreover, because these are contextual spaces, The Figure also expresses *the perception of how potential unfolds from the vantage point of 63 different positionalities or contexts.*

The 63 contextual spaces are organized into 7 different levels, or hierarchies of space. The levels are interconnected, and, as the lines of The Figure suggest, there is no space that is disconnected from another. Another way of expressing this observation, is to say that there is an underlying unity that is never lost, since every context with its potentials is connected to the overall potential of The Figure.

The unity of The Figure is a symbol of the nonlinear common ground of Being that is the divine potential for, and within, every human life. For many people, it is expressed in the familiar words in the book of Genesis. In the symbolism of the tool, The Figure is an abstraction of the process of the unmanifest becoming manifest, which is taking place, simultaneously, on all scales, large or small, microscopic or macroscopic, local or global, individual or universal, physical or spiritual.

Therefore, The Figure may be used to represent the process for any scope or type of manifestation, whether it be a cell, a human, the solar system, or beyond. The guiding intuition is the belief that all is connected by a common process, and the Presence of the Creator is in everything, at every level of complexity. Matter is not dead, or inert, but alive, possessing its own form of consciousness, because there is no restriction of the Divine Presence. The perspective of *divine transcendence* underlies the belief in a hierarchy and underlying uniformity of purpose that is intrinsic to the universe, regardless of context, a so-called "top to bottom" formulation. The essence of the Presence is also in the universe, including the human experience, as *divine immanence*, a "bottom to the top" perspective.

The Figure invites exploration of the highest frame of reference that one might imagine. The Figure awakens new possibilities to consider the relationship between the bio-body suit at every level of organization and the spiritual laws of creation. The experience of what is called *karma* may be connected to the unfolding of the Unmanifest in time space as emotional, mental, and spiritual incoherencies, represented by precise locations on the contextual map. *Below* the physical structure, or, if you like, *within* its structure, or, *moving through* the structure, there is a hierarchical information structure of awareness.

Seven Primary Contextual Spaces

There are seven primary triangles which symbolize seven primary contextual spaces and forms of human coherence. Three questions immediately come to mind: What is the relationship between the seven primary triangles? What is the significance of their locations and orientations relative to each other? What may be said about the origin of the seven primary "parts" of the tool?

<u>What is the relationship between the seven primary triangles?</u>

Based on IBFRT findings, the relationship between the seven primary triangles may be interpreted as hierarchical. This determination is based on the correlation between different types of incoherence identified with IBFRT and the matching of the type of coherence with a primary triangle. These findings generate a hierarchy that begins with physical coherence and ends with spiritual coherence. Primary Triangle One is reflective of physical coherence. Therefore, physical incoherence is found by IBFRT as a stressful response to one or more of the nine triangles in Primary Triangle One. Primary Triangle Two reflects emotional coherence. Primary Triangles Three, Four, and Five are connected with mental coherence. The distinctions between Primary Triangles Three, Four, and Five correlate with different levels of consciousness in the Hawkins Map of Consciousness (MOC). Primary Triangle Three corresponds with the MOC levels 1 to 199. Primary Triangle Four corresponds with the levels from 200 to 499 on the MOC. Primary Triangle Five corresponds with MOC levels from 500 to 599. The qualities of consciousness within these ranges will be discussed when the contents of the triangles are described. Primary Triangle Six is connected with spiritual coherence including individual karmic spiritual coherence. The correspondence with the MOC is the state of non-duality from 600 to 850. Primary Triangle Seven reflects the highest forms of human spiritual coherence including complete enlightenment. The MOC numbers for the final primary triangle are 851 to 1000. The innermost triangle within Primary Triangle Seven is triangle 63 which corresponds to 1000 on the MOC.

<u>What is the significance of their locations and orientation relative to each other?</u>

The picture of The Figure symbolizes a progression, or evolution of consciousness, from the physical to the spiritual. The vertices of the two spiritual primary triangles (six and seven), located within the five non-spiritual triangles (one through five), point downward while the five vertices of the non-spiritual triangles point upward. The words from the New Testament come to mind, that "we have this treasure in an earthen vessel"—or Dr. Tiller's words—that "we are spiritual beings having a physical experience"—come to mind when studying the locations and overall significance of each primary triangle which creates The Figure. Looking at The Figure in its entirety as a symbol of consciousness, the design of The Figure is evocative of Dr. Tiller's working hypothesis that "consciousness is an emergent quality of the interaction of spirit with matter." The Figure also symbolizes the participation in consciousness by placing the contexts of permanence, the eternal "world" of spirit within, yet hidden to most levels of human consciousness, that are potentially experienced between the space of thoughts, feelings, and sensations. These are the contexts of impermanence that surround the core of The Figure.

What may be said about the origin of the seven primary "parts" of the tool?

Just a few paragraphs ago, I described the origin of the tool.

I wrote: "Where does the tool come from? The tool which I refer to as The Figure comes from another realm of meaningful primary reality that transcends time and space. So then, what about the seven primary parts? Is it like buying a car manufactured in the United States and finding out that the parts have been made in factories throughout the world?"

The seven primary triangles, including the nine triangles within each primary triangle, are also created by consciousness. The best answer is the simple one. Consciousness is free to create, within the scope of consciousness symbolized by The Figure, anything it chooses! There is a location or dimension created by consciousness in which a differentiated aspect of consciousness governs the manifestation of what is perceived to be physical (sensations) such as objects, qualities, properties, or physical laws. There will be another location or dimension within consciousness, that is partitioned by consciousness, to govern the manifestation of emotional objects (feelings), still another for different categories of mental objects (thoughts), and still other contextual spaces for spiritual objects (fields). Consciousness creates and assembles all of the tools that it needs or wishes to create to accomplish any intention. Consciousness uses these tools to construct and interpret itself, and what it has created including concrete reality. The process is never ending because it is the nature of consciousness to evolve.

The tools of whisperology are created in a realm of consciousness that includes all of the parts (triangles) of The Figure.

Context Heals Content
Every triangle in The Figure symbolizes a different contextual space. The perimeter of the triangle determines the perceptual limitations of the person who lives within its boundaries. Through the person's conscious and unconscious powers of perception, he or she selects objects and experiences from an infinite supply of sensations, emotions, and thoughts to include within what is regarded as the "real world." The particular triangle in which one resides is the primary filter that determines what is essential, trivial, or invisible. The primary determinant of what the filter is capturing and ignoring is based on the level of consciousness, and the coherence of consciousness, within the triangle.

The filtering process is only somewhat voluntary. Much of the selection is governed by rules that are unknown and unexamined unless the person is expanding consciousness through some form of integrous spiritual practice. The truth is that most of the time, human beings are in charge of very little of the world they believe to be the source of sustenance and reality. Despite all of the stressful and relentless efforts to control the contents of life, the only way to change the trajectory of a human life is to stop acting as if fear is the only way to stay alive. Decisive change occurs through a single mechanism called recontextualization. The Figure expresses this truth very plainly: one lives in a new triangle in which perception operates according to a more expansive filter.

The content of life changes at the moment when *perception is given a new filter*. Why might you experience stress differently than someone else? Because you occupy a different triangle. The perceptions that appear to make sense in your triangle may be very different than any other person. The context in which you perceive and interpret what you sense, feel, and think is *an expression of your context*. The filters that determine what is included and what is excluded, consciously and unconsciously, are a reflection of the particular triangle you call home.

The Figure symbolizes that only a selective group of perceptions are included within a particular space. The perceptions may be regarded as objects, or events, which capture our attention, and remain within the field of awareness. There will be "objects" of various kinds: physical objects, feeling objects, thought objects. All of these objects are embodied forms of intention that carry energy. One could say that each of us has our own particular affinity for some of these objects, while there are others that we avoid, or we believe have no connection or relevance to our experience. The objects for which we have a strong affinity are the basis of our perceptual field, the context of our life, and the choice of which objects are included within our awareness is the basis of the particular type and level of consciousness through which we experience life.

The Figure also expresses an important principle about the connections *between* different types of objects. Each type of object is connected with a different type of *primary* triangle space. For example, physical objects belong to one of the nine spaces in Primary Triangle One whereas emotional objects belong to one of the nine triangles in

Primary Triangle Two. These are linked and influenced most importantly by the overall level of consciousness which is represented by the triangle which encapsulates an overall level of consciousness. The different aspects of our being are hierarchically related. The Figure describes the experience of living in several contextual *planes* at once. In Eastern thought, one is considered to have several subtle bodies not just a physical body. The Figure expresses a similar conception.

What more may be said about the relationship between the objects and the space that is connected with them? This is a bit tricky. The analogy of a "getting out of the box" has its limitations with exactly this question. The space is not unlike a physical box in the sense that a box is a container to keep stuff inside of it. *The space within the triangle, its "contents," is the unmanifested space in which the objects are created, not a collection of things.* The space within a particular triangle can only manifest within it the objects that belong within that space. One might compare the space to an incubator which furnishes the right environment to not only hatch the egg but welcome the egg to appear from an invisible hen! Once the eggs are hatched, the objects still belong to the space from which each of them operated. The object, as the manifestation of an intention of some aspect of consciousness, is inseparable from the original intention which brought it from the space in which it was given birth. Therefore, the object is an *emergent quality of the space*.

Physical objects are probably the hardest to understand in this fashion because we regard them as "things." However, physical consciousness has no separate independent existence from consciousness and the space "incubator" that is powered by intention. Remember: We are not reducible to a physical substance because we are essentially spiritual beings having a physical experience. Physical objects are a necessary part of the mechanism for consciousness to experience life in a body. How does this physical experience arise within consciousness? Consciousness creates space including a form, or dimension, of *space in which the consciousness of physical space is included.* The consciousness of physical space, a form of unmanifested space, is the creative incubator of physical objects, the manifestation of all the qualities of the physical objects including the physical objects themselves.

While all of us, as spiritual beings, are having a physical experience, for one person the perception may be as bleak as being trapped in a prison with no way out, and for another, there is the joyful bliss of being surrounded by a completely different set of objects that are experienced as a peaceful garden. The interconnection between the triangles from each space as it relates specifically to an individual will be discussed in a later chapter.

Stress and Incoherence

Stress is a form of incoherence. The inability to move beyond the limitations with the existing content of a particular space will create stress *on every level* for the individual. This stress is reflected in a loss of coherence in every contextual plane that comprises the human. When there is stress—in whatever form, physical or spiritual—*the symbolism of the two triangles offers two possible solutions to reduce or eliminate the problem.*

The first solution is to restore or increase the coherence of the primary context in which the human resides by expanding or modifying the content within the existing belief system. An increase of coherence within the current context allows the new or improved content to satisfy certain "problems" without recontextualization (moving to a different triangle).

The second solution is a higher resolution of the problem because the stress is transcended through a paradigm shift. The new context is a different space (a different triangle) in which the content of a less-conscious context develops a new meaning within a more conscious context that transforms the old "problems." The change from a smaller context to a larger context may be considered to be an evolution of consciousness. Qualitative change is possible with an expansion of context.

David Hawkins expresses the power of a contextual shift in the following way: "The difference between treating and healing is that in the former the context remains the same, whereas I the latter the clinical response is elicited by a change of context, so as to bring about an absolute removal of the cause of the condition rather than mere recovery from its symptoms. It is one thing to prescribe and anti-hypertensive medication for high blood pressure. It is quite another to expand the patient's context of life so he stops being angry and repressive."[138]

IBFRT offers a means to observe the relationship between context and content. When stress is defined as incoherence, then it is possible to differentiate stress into different types of incoherence: spiritual, karmic, mental, emotional, and physical. The consideration of each type of incoherence is connected to a specific lack of coherence within a particular contextual space. Resolution of stress is possible when incoherence is removed through either approach.

The migration to a new triangle is symbolic of the power of intention and divine grace to enter into a new level of expanded spiritual awareness and manifestation of unrealized human potential.

All Space is Connected

I also realized and confirmed that when the correct triangle is chosen and its coherency increased, there is a positive impact on every other triangle. Since all areas are connected and united in the divine image that is present in all things, great and small, it only makes sense, doesn't it? The areas within the same group are especially benefited. It is also very interesting that those areas that are in the same relative spatial relationship within a different group benefit more than the others in a dif-

---

[138] Hawkins, David R. *Power vs Force* (Veritas Publishing, Sedona, Arizona: 1995), p. 57.

ferent group. For example, when the coherency of triangle four in Primary Triangle One is increased, the coherency of triangle thirteen in Primary Triangle Two is increased more than the other triangles in Primary Triangle Two. The effects extend through the entire system including triangle twenty-two in Primary Triangle Three—and beyond! Again, you see the symmetry: $22 - 13 = 9$ and $13 - 4 = 9$. The number 9 has a way of showing up, every now and again, in the world of whisperology.

A number of intriguing directions of inquiry have been hinted at so far. Lots of homework assignments! And now I smile and think of the words of my friend. Of course, as Bill reminded me, "It is possible that the seven groups of triangles could be used as symbols for anything one can imagine."

PART II. TOOL APPLICATION

CHAPTER FOUR
Core Beliefs and Guiding Principles

Before the two approaches to using the new tool are illustrated, let us summarize the core beliefs and guiding principles of whisperology. Using IBFRT, a series of statements was developed and confirmed (given a "passing grade" by the Inner Teacher) that would best describe the new developments in whisperology that have come as a consequence of adding The Figure to the toolbox.

The Figure symbolizes qualities, or spiritual elements, of the Divine Essence.

The Figure is a representation of the spiritual realms through which the 63 Divine Governing Presences are expressed.

The qualities of the Divine Essence are manifested from the Unmanifest through alignment with The Field. The infinite manifests in the finite and loses awareness of its essence because it operates within a finite world until it returns home.

Through alignment with the unconditional field of Love, humans manifest all 63 qualities of the Divine Essence.

Every entity manifests one or more of the qualities of the Divine Essence. All qualities in every entity come from the Divine Essence but not all of them are expressed in every entity (rocks, bacteria, plants, fish, birds, mammals, etc.). These qualities are manifested through different aspects of The Field.

To be made in the image and likeness of the Creator is to be given the potential to express all 63 qualities of the Divine Essence through alignment with The Field which manifests the gifts of the Spirit. This is the perfect expression of the finite realizing that the infinite is its abiding reality and presence.

Each quality (element, gift, level, space) of the Divine Essence, creates its manifestation of coherence, consciousness, and awareness through alignment with The Field.

Every contextual field is contained within The Figure and has its particular misperceptions, which may include physical, emotional, mental, karmic, and spiritual incoherencies. The Field is the eternal and infinite field of awareness itself. The contextual fields are not imperfect but incomplete in the sense that these spaces are objects which manifest in the finite realm only an aspect or portion of full awareness, that is, the eternal Field. Each of these objects is created and governed by the principles which are responsible for its creation in consciousness.

Primary triangles one through seven symbolize levels of infinite space *in* which, *through* which, and *with* which different forms of awareness are expressed as universal objects of human experience.

All spaces and primary triangles are an abstraction of what is an indivisible whole.

The purpose, composition, and application of The Figure expands the implications of these fundamental statements.

Tool Maximization

How may the tool be used to be of the greatest help to others? By always asking for God's guidance from a place of integrous intention.

The Figure opens up the possibility of new insights about the different qualities of human "experiencing" instead of settling for a conventional idea of what it means to be healthy, from a singular physically based model.

The relationships between the seven primary triangles form the basis for the two uses of the tool. Seven primary triangles locate seven primary contexts of human experience. There is the most recognized perception of physical experience in the physical body. However, there are other contexts, or "bodies," that are not perceived by most people that may be described as subtle but are no less real than the physical one! In whisperology, and in the Eastern traditions, there are emotional "bodies," mental "bodies," and spiritual "bodies." These other bodies are intrinsically linked with the physical body *but are not produced by the physical body*. All of the bodies, not only the physical body, may be whispered to using either approach.

There are several ways to work with the triangles to identify incoherent conditions that create health concerns. One approach is based on what we may know about a health problem from a conventional physically based understanding, and is more consistent with the first method of using The Figure. The second approach moves in an unconventional direction because recontextualization of a health problem often places what has been perceived to be a physical problem within a non-physical context.

With either approach, when the areas of incoherence are located within The Figure, the conditions are treated through numerical sequences and the methods of whisperology. IBFRT determines which approach should be taken, however, the two approaches eventually lead to the same destination because there is no *essential* health which does not include the integration of body, mind, and spirit.

The Figure allows one to discover and appreciate the connections between these different aspects of health by comparing the incoherent spaces between the primary triangles. IBFRT also identifies and confirms the influence of one primary triangle upon the other primary triangles, or in other words, how the body is subject to what is being held in mind within a particular contextual space. Limited perception experiences the appearance of seven primary triangles as connected but distinguishable forms when the essential Human is a formless, indivisible whole that includes the cosmos. These beliefs are similar to many of the theories in Eastern thought.

The relationship between spiritual and physical incoherence was discussed and illustrated in the second book of the series in Chapter 10 about Morgan's friend, Allan. With the addition of the new tool, there is a deepened understanding of Allan's response to whisperology which will hopefully become evident through the examples shared in this book.

I realize that if you have not worked with me, that it is still probably hard for you to imagine what an H vial is, or how it is used to develop the meanings within The Figure. I included a brief overview of some of these developments at the start of the book. You may find, however, that reading all of my books will help you to overcome this obstacle. The concept of "matching" might help to shed some light on the subject. When incoherence, regardless of the type of incoherence is measured, I use IBFRT to sense the lack of coherence through the reception of a stress response in my hands. I hold the stress response regarding a particular incoherence in mind until I find the space—the triangle—from which it originated. I feel the stress disappear as it recognizes its origin, the space that holds it. In other words, the stress response of the incoherence (that arises from a lack of coherence between content and context) is matched to its space. Does that help?

The same process of matching is used to identify each form of incoherence with its correct level (primary triangle) and the space within that level. *The result is a beautiful picture of interlocking triangles through which the actual becomes potential, a series of realizations, not causal connections, but stages of evolution in every level of the human experience.* Using The Figure to describe the various levels of awareness that *move through* the human being, and the degree of coherence for any particular contextual space, creates a new map of a person, at any point in his or her life, *within or outside of space time, or you might say, pre- and post-Incarnation.* The Figure becomes a powerful map to assess spiritual and physical incoherence and target intentions using the numerical sequences, a tool of magnification. This enhances the ability to specify the destination of a whisper, know something about the rules of the neighborhood in which the recipient lives (the context), and monitor how well the message was received and understood (change of coherence). Collapsing time, from past, present, and future, into "timeless experiencing" (a qualitatively different form of awareness) by using The Figure, changes the incoherence that the ego has attached to its concepts about time (limiting beliefs about the perceived past or future) when imprinting is targeted to one of these conceptual obstacles.

Using IBFRT and the tools of whisperology matched each one of the seven primary triangles (levels, bodies, or informational structures) with a type of incoherence. Once these hierarchical relationships between the spaces were established, the exploration of these contextual spaces was undertaken to investigate the emergence of content with a particular person and the human experience called life. With a new map in hand, the time was right to learn more about the influence of a magnified whisper that recognized, more directly, the context of the whisperee.

IBFRT was also used to identify the relationships between elements and The Figure. See Figure 5. "Correlation Of Elements With The Figure" in the Appendix. The Figure and the associated elements are used to explore another context which I call "elemental coherence."

Elemental Coherence

What is Elemental Coherence? Elemental coherence means being coherent with a naturally occurring element from the periodic table of elements. The man-made elements of the periodic table are not included. Elemental coherence is based on the *belief* that each element is not fully described according to its physical structure and physical-chemical properties. Every element originates from a non-linear (spiritual) domain which is not accessible or fully understood by its physical qualities and behaviors.

Each element has a particular essence, including elemental consciousness. For this reason, the element is a spiritual element. The physical aspects which are observable in the linear domain of space time, are a manifestation of its essence. Elemental coherence is another way of exploring the coherence between humans and the rest of creation at a more fundamental level.

Elemental coherence expands the context of interconnectivity between human beings and the environment. The environment includes the external environment outside the bio-body suit, as Dr. Tiller frequently referred to the human body, and the internal environment within its structures. The external environment includes the land, water, earth, moon, planets, and sun. Perhaps one could simply say the intention is to include all of the elements which comprise the universe. The internal environment includes all of the organisms and other substances which reside within the bio-body suit and are typically considered to not be human but animate (parasites, bacteria, yeast, etc.), as well as what is regarded as inanimate and usually toxic, or not essential, for human life (lead, titanium, osmium, etc.)

The belief that elemental coherence is an important context is based on the belief that human health and the evolution of human consciousness is advanced through an expanded context, or awareness, of a unity with everything that is manifested in space time. This includes an appreciation and deepening of the connections between all aspects of creation at an elemental level.

Whisperology intends to amplify the interconnections through harmonious alignment with all the elements at a spiritual and energetic level. In this context, there are not good elements and bad elements—only coherent and incoherent alignments. In this context, for example, there are not good and bad bacteria. Germ theory or immune defense theories are superseded by the belief in bacterial coherence. Bacteria are not the target of destruction, but an alteration of elemental coherence brings peaceful coexistence with mutual benefits.

From a different positionality, The Figure is an abstraction of the element itself. The belief is that there appear to be 63 different contexts for each element. When a particular element is held in consciousness while doing IBFRT, The Figure reveals the incoherencies for that particular element. Change the element that is held in mind, and The Figure reveals the incoherent locations for that element. Elemental coherence for each element is reflected in particular triangles, but not all of them. A helpful analogy to consider the coherence differences for one element within The Figure is to think about how the properties of an element are modified by its physical environment. For example, the context of iron is different in a blood cell, or an iron utilizing enzyme, or a car, a rock, or a bacterium. There is evidence from the testing that increasing coherence with iron also increases emotional, mental, and spiritual coherence through an elemental recontextualization which is not understood or explicable in chemical terms. My impression is that these beliefs which imply a form of elemental consciousness probably do not reflect Hawkins or Tiller. My belief is that what is regarded as just matter is not inert but only appears to be lifeless.

Elemental coherence is an aspect of coherence to be explored–with permission. When David Hawkins described the Map of Consciousness (MOC), he reminded his audience that the MOC was an abstraction, that is, a teaching tool. The MOC was "not the same as the reality to which it refers. It also appears to artificially separate that which is a wholeness and a continuum into seemingly distinct partitions based on identifiable characteristics. The calibrated levels represent a perspective, an arbitrary point of observation, which is significant only in relation to the whole."[139]

Elemental coherence and The Figure are helpful teaching, testing, and treatment tools which are tied to a positionality and an abstraction, which is believed to be useful for consciousness to know itself in certain aspects. Hawkins writes, "Consciousness at its highest frequencies permits awareness beyond the linear physical to self-revelations of its essence, yet at the lowest frequencies, it is insufficient to even support physical life, which then sickens and dies in exhaustion and apathy."[140] Elemental Coherence appears to be a positionality that is reflective of a consciousness that is aligned with a high frequency spiritual awareness which is impersonal. The high frequency is awakened in others through testing and imprinting.

There are other positionalities, also abstractions, which may reflect higher levels of awareness and activation of still higher frequencies that could be described by words like "sub-elemental coherence" or "universal coherence."

Before sharing any examples of using The Figure to address specific health problems, I must introduce two additional topics that are relevant to the subject of tool maximization: first, the division of triangles into sub-triangles, and secondly, a unit of measurement that I call a deltope.

Subdivision of Triangles

The Figure consists of 63 triangles. What about these triangles? May these triangles be partitioned into smaller triangles? The answer is

---

[139] Hawkins, *I: Reality and Subjectivity*, p. 343
[140] Ibid, p. 344

yes, of course. Is the subdivision into smaller triangles helpful? Quite possibly, yes!

For example, what if I would like to triangulate the location of a problem, or incoherence, even more exactly? The division of the areas into even smaller areas identifies a more precise location to correlate a triangular subspace with a particular object (stress, physical structure, etc.) that is being monitored, before and after imprinting.

Does a smaller space improve the imprinting outcomes because the target size is reduced? The question is, at the very least, intriguing. Subdivision of triangles is a promising approach to making new discoveries about how smaller areas of space contain a smaller set of objects, structures, and events, which are linked not by causal connection, but rather through a process of contextual sphere which is currently unknown. New connections between structures and events which don't make sense in the current medical model may become evident within the larger contextual frameworks of consciousness that contain physical or spiritual conditions.

The triangles may be partitioned an infinite number of times. The partition follows a pattern of division which continues to generate smaller and smaller representations of The Figure. This occurs because of the alternating pattern of partitioning the space first into seven triangles and then the division of each of the seven newly created triangles into nine triangles. 63 x 7 = 441 triangles. 441 x 9 = 3969 triangles. Or, 63 x 63 = 3969 triangles. The division could continue until when, infinity? Yes. 63 x 63 x 63 x 63 x.... To the point that every space contains only a single event, a single object. The Figure becomes smaller but does not lose its fundamental shape as a geometric representation of the presence of the Creator in every bit of the universe, no matter how large or small, how complex or simple.

There is a deep spiritual symbolism expressed in the isosceles triangle. Consider the birth of a single triangle of infinitely small proportions. Beginning with a point called the origination point, intention is born in the location that will become the upper vertex of the triangle. This is the beginning of the event. One can imagine two vectors of identical strength and direction, called volition and discernment, leaving the origin, the upper vertex. The two vectors represent the perfect balance of love and wisdom. These vectors, equipped with the perfect force and direction, stop at precisely the same time. Then the two vectors are instantaneously linked at their destination by a horizontal line. The event, or event potential, is located within the space inside of the miniscule triangle. The three lines of the triangle create a *contextual boundary* that separates this event from any other event. While every event in space time appears to be unique and "personal," events that share a similar context, are grouped together in one of the 63 "impersonal" triangular spaces according to the rules which govern the overall context of the space. If looked at in reverse, from the standpoint of The Figure, the structure apprehends the entire unfolding of creation as a constellation of events that evolve within a particular context, *and level of awareness*. Subdivision of the 63 triangular spaces into smaller spaces creates greater specificity of context (a smaller space). A nearly infinite number of subdivisions would be required to reduce the space of the triangle to a size that included only a single event.

What does whisperology have to do with subdivision of The Figure into smaller areas that also carry the structure of The Figure? The relevance is based on the interest in contrasting the qualities and efficacy of sending a specific versus a general intention. The sending of intention to the correct location moves from the general to the specific. First, one of the seven primary triangles are identified. Secondly, one of the nine triangles within the chosen primary triangle is identified. At this point, one triangle is matched to the "problem" and 62 triangles have been set aside for consideration as the target of the whisper. Dividing the remaining triangle, first by seven triangles, and then each of the seven triangles into nine triangles, creates 63 new spaces. The selection of one of these triangles means that one space has been chosen for imprinting and 63 x

63 − 1 = 3968 spaces are set aside. This is a much more precise location within The Figure! Another division of the remaining space will create a single space that is distinguished from 63 x 63 x 63 − 1 = 250,046 spaces! The numbers get big in a hurry. *With each division of the space into smaller spaces, the location of the problem, or event, becomes more exact.* The smallest areas open new areas of understanding about the relationships between incoherent conditions in these more closely defined areas as a function of time and location.

This is a very interesting subject that reveals new findings whenever the division of The Figure method is used.

Deltopes

Deltopes? What is a deltope? Let me try to explain.

There is a unit of measurement for nearly everything. Pounds, inches, watts, pennies, bits, and so on. Why not a unit of measurement for intention? How could I assess the power or intensity of intention? I was interested in creating a means to measure it during the imprinting process, as well as consider what might be done to increase the power and efficacy of imprinting.

I used IBFRT to develop a name for a unit of measurement for intention. As described previously, with the guidance of the Inner Teacher, I recorded, letter by letter, a name for the unit. The name that was generated was deltope. The name immediately connected to Bill Tiller's work and the postulated deltron substance which connects etheric and physical substances together. [141] I more than smiled at the similarity. I also was reminded that delta is the symbol for the capital letter in the Greek language which is written as an isosceles triangle. I also thought about the compatibility of the new word *deltope* with the well-known term *decibel* that measures the intensity of a sound. Now there was a term for the intensity of a whisper!

---

[141] Tiller, *Science and Human Transformation*, p. 84

I decided to build an arbitrary scale from 1 to 100, of deltopes per moment of intention, to measure deltope generation during a particular activity. 1 is the smallest amount of deltopes per moment required to intend any activity. 100 is the maximum amount of deltopes per moment possible that a human being is able to generate for any intention generated activity. Then, I used IBFRT to determine the maximum number of deltopes per moment generated by various individuals performing different tasks.

What fun! What food for thought! Here are a few of the findings:

Jesus generated 100 deltopes per moment. Mother Theresa over 50 deltopes per moment. The best professional athletes in the world—highly disciplined and well trained with ability to concentrate attention and maximize the efficiency of their bodies—generated about 15 deltopes per moment. It didn't matter if it was driving a race car over 200 mph, converting the winning free throw when the clock had expired, or throwing a baseball over the plate at 90 mph in the 9th inning. A measly 15 deltopes!

The compelling explanation, verified by IBFRT, is that the deltopes per moment is based on the level of consciousness of the deltope generator, the one that is building the intention. The contextual field of love generates a whisper heard throughout the universe that is a more powerful field than the sound in any sports arena. This realization underscores the connection between consciousness and the power of intention. The secret to generating a healing field with as many deltopes per moment as humanly possible will be found in the heart, not the gym or playing field. The intensity of intention is activated by grace through the healing intentions of "the intender." Anyone—anyone!—may become a powerful sender of loving intention, a deltope professional!

This arbitrary, but very useful, scale highlights the power of prayer and loving intention. When asked how the deltopes may be further increased in each moment, additional guidance was available. The most important finding is that nothing is personal. Nothing. If you would like to increase the output of deltopes, then, get the ego out of the way! Don't make it about yourself; what you need, or what you think you have to offer. Remember, it's not personal. Ask only for God to author the intention to magnify love.

Deltope production also increases through numerical sequences that clarify and focus attention on a particular integrous target of intention. Numbers and numerical sequences also may carry the Creator's purpose. The particular number, the arrangement of the numbers into a sequence, and their alignment, magnifies the power of intention. The sequence delivers the whisper to the intended receiver. Using a sequence is like sending a letter and being certain it will reach its destination if it includes the name of the recipient and mailing address. A group of people focused on the same target of intention through prayer or meditation also increases deltope production.

By far, the most important factor is for the imprinter to intend that he or she be aligned with all of creation, with heavenly beings, and with the power of the Spirit. Healing happens through the imprinter by letting go of any notion that one is special or gifted. At best, the imprinter is a conduit, a vehicle of the grace of the Great Unseen, and therefore, a catalyst for healing. The energy field of the healer is powerful but it does not belong to him or her. Humility opens the floodgate to very high levels of deltope production during imprinting.

Focus not only mentally but visually on the particular triangle that you are interacting with through your intention when using the numerical sequence to restore coherence. Visualization while developing the sequences and imprinting the sequences is powerful. Besides focusing on the numerical sequence, imagine that the entire area is being restored. The original, eternal, and complete space replaces the present, past, and future space. Use your imagination to see the space become coherent by focusing attention on its perfect symmetry and shape, or by seeing it filled with light, or by seeing it be transformed to its original color and state of perfection. There are many possibilities, more than I will ever know, or will possibly fathom.

Sometimes I receive feedback from the person that describes the experience of imprinting as seeing colors like purple and gold, including the elimination of black. Interesting, isn't it? The governing idea behind area restoration is that the space is aligned through intention with the image and likeness of the Creator and the spiritual laws of the Creator.

CHAPTER FIVE
Seven Primary Triangles

The Figure comes from a particular level of consciousness, and is understood to be an abstraction of the objects of body, mind, and spirit *within consciousness. Moreover, these objects are created by consciousness to know itself.* Using the whisperology tools, the following description of each primary triangle was developed. There are many different words that will appear in the book to describe the contents and the relationships between the seven primary triangles. *The most conscious descriptions of these seven spaces is to regard each space as a structure of awareness within consciousness.*

The seven primary triangles, and the nine triangles within each of the primary triangles, are also symbolically related to a particular element of the periodic table. The connection with the element appears to reflect not only the physical properties or characteristics which are known by chemistry, but also its metaphysical, or spiritual connections with Human and cosmos. The connection, or correspondence, between the element and a particular space includes information about the "spiritual" element. The physical properties of an element will be part of the

...tivity in which the spiritual element is manifested within a particular space to know itself. Consciousness about the element aligns with the governing metaphysical laws of the space that is objectified by two parallel processes; the assignment of the name of the element to a space, and the governing presence within the space.

Imprinted vials, which I refer to as H Vials, were used to identify the overall structure of The Figure, the associated element, and the nature of events and objects which are connected with each space, or in other words, with that level of awareness. The H Vials that are being used to explore the seven primary triangles are imprinted to identify incoherencies of different types including physical, emotional, mental, karmic (collective and personal), and spiritual.

Primary Triangle One.

Every *physical* structure in the body, at every level of organization, is located in Primary Triangle One. This includes atoms and biomolecules, as well as complex structures like cells, organs, and tissues. These structures are composed of an infinite number of physical objects which appear in the perceptual field of time space. Every physical object is a manifestation of the unmanifest which originates with an intention that unfolds with an event which incarnates the event as an object, but as Hawkins repeatedly emphasized, not as a chain of causal reactions.

The content of physical incoherence is the most differentiated or realized level of development in space time. Regardless of the type or degree of physical incoherence, in any person, the *contents* of physical incoherence will always be found in one of the nine *contexts* inside of the first primary triangle. Using IBFRT, the Primary Triangle One location has been verified hundreds of times, with many different test subjects of different ages and degrees of health, to investigate and treat those aspects of human experience, which appear to be the most resistant to change, the most anchored in the "historical past," and associated with the manifested object called the body.

The body is the earthen vessel which allows us to experience what most of us call "being alive." As such, the body appears to be our most precious possession. The loss or impairment of bodily functions is connected with the deepest fears of survival and impermanence. A common belief about the body is that the destiny of the body is exclusively, or primarily determined by the genes, a seemingly fixed unmovable blessing or curse of genetic instructions. The genes that one is dealt will be a determinative factor of an entire life, depending more on the cards you were dealt than the way you played them. You are either lucky or a hopeless victim. If you listen to the way in which people reflect about life then you will likely hear many references to good or bad luck including the health of the body.

The perception of the body is that while it changes over time according to well identified stages of growth and deterioration, there is limited influence over its vitality. Fear about its function fuels lifestyle experiments and trips to the medical specialists. One lives in fear that someday, after some dreaded exam, the doctor will tell you the grim news that you have an incurable disease like cancer.

Past physical traumas, including neonatal trauma, are always located within one of the nine spaces of the first primary triangle. The popular conception of trauma is reinforced by the commonly held limiting belief of the victim whose fate has been determined by accidents and unjust events which are beyond his or her control. The person feels subject to the body as the essential requirement to achieve a personal goal, and, at other times, a prison from which there is no hope of recovery.

Primary Triangle One is perceived to be defined by those physical objects and events which appear to operate with the smallest amount of freedom or consciousness, and are thereby considered to belong to the lowest structures of awareness. The level of consciousness is so low that the structures are considered by most experts to be completely unconscious structures of awareness that simply and invariably obey unbreakable laws like the classical laws of thermodynamics or Maxwell's equations.

In space time, every entity has at least this minimal level of awareness. The common quality at this level of awareness is the innate capacity and intention to survive, and to behave within the local conditions in a manner that preserves identity, or self-sameness. The will to survive and to preserve identity is present not only in people but animals, plants, bacteria, even rocks. Could one expand the group to include an atom or molecule? All of life shares a common identity and awareness, a quality of physicality, that is usually perceived to be subject to little, or no change.

On a very small scale, the elements of the periodic table are symbolized in The Figure. The essence, or fundamental identity of the element, occupies a particular space. I believe that it is helpful to appreciate that the Creator bestows each element with a form of elemental consciousness. My view about elemental consciousness appears to be somewhat different from Hawkins. David Hawkins describes the difference between life and inert matter in *I: Reality and Subjectivity*, the last book of his trilogy, where he writes:

"Matter is analogous to a copper wire that is inert and has no actual function until an electric current courses through it at which time it becomes a 'live wire.'"[142] He adds, "'Life' has a quality, a completely different essence, capacity, and 'characteristic' from inert material. It is not even in the same class or category as materiality."[143]

When I dissected Hawkins' statements, using IBFRT, I reached a somewhat different conclusion about the relationship between life and "inert matter;" that matter is analogous to a copper wire not because it is inert or has no actual function. I don't agree with the belief that copper

---

[142] Hawkins, *I: Reality and Subjectivity*, p. 403.
[143] Ibid.

is adequately described as an inert material, if inert is defined as inanimate, static, or an unmoving substance. I don't believe that copper has the power of self-determination to determine its context. However, IBFRT does support the belief that copper learns, modifies, and adapts to many different contexts because it possesses a different form of consciousness. Furthermore, human consciousness through the power of intention can change the context and content of copper.

The interaction between human intention and the physical world has been proven by Bill Tiller. Water is generally considered to be a substance without consciousness or awareness, and yet it holds information that is imprinted into its "inert" matrix through many methods. Human intention to raise or lower pH may be held by a Tiller-invented device, the device sent to a laboratory thousands of miles away, and perform its pH changing "magic" on water. Bill describes the human body as the bio-body suit. I believe that there is value in considering the notion that human life and human experience are not simply *taking place within the bio-body suit but human experience is the outcome of Spirit flowing through the bio-body suit.* Using Hawkins analogy of the live wire in this conception is a highly coherent formulation of the dynamic activity called living. I simply want to emphasize that the bio-body suit is also an expression of the divine essence and is alive and responsive to the rest of creation including human intention.

When I began working with the periodic table, I developed sequences for each element. My understanding of the elements has evolved with the use of The Figure. Copper, for example, *when considered from the context of its essence instead of one its physical forms* (elemental copper, copper ion, a particular isotope of copper, or compounds containing copper) is matched to a context in Primary Triangle Seven, the inner group of triangles, as a spiritual element within consciousness. The manifestation of copper occurs within thousands of different contexts (in a rock, a plant, a human cell, an enzyme, and so on) in which its content is determined by the context. *However, copper also is connected with a particular gift of the Spirit.* Incoherence of copper appears to reflect an analogous incoherence with a particular spiritual gift. Or, is it the other way around?

The relationship between the elements and the triangles in The Figure is depicted in Figure 5. "Correlation Of The Elements With The Figure." The use of the elements to test and imprint "elemental coherence" is discussed in Chapter 4.

Primary Triangle One is most subject to the illusions of materialism and the belief that all that is real, and therefore, reliable, is matter. The dominant perception is that only matter exists and everything is discoverable through a matter-based expertise about the world and ourselves. IBFRT identifies a *connection between Primary Triangle One and the spiritual element iron.*

Besides those physical structures which are identified as human, all of the other physical entities, such as microbes, are found in the first primary triangle. *Regardless of the specifics of the physical incoherence, IBFRT always identifies that the incoherencies between Human and microbe include connections within the first level, that is, Primary Triangle One.*

Primary Triangle Two.

IBFRT identifies in the second primary triangle the locations, or contexts, of emotional objects. It is commonly said that one should get control of oneself and it is generally believed that humans have it in their power to choose an emotional state. In the midst of strong emotions, however, one might be inclined to say that the emotions have us! There does at least appear to be a significantly greater degree of freedom and adaptability about feelings although there is a different set of laws at work, which affect the ways in which emotions are experienced or managed. IBFRT indicates that there is some portion of the response to environmental stress that seems to engage the emotions with the same discretion that is shared with plants, not rocks. Do plants have feelings?

I wouldn't put it quite that way and will leave it to others to weigh the merits of this belief. When IBFRT identifies Emotional Incoherence, the location always matches, or includes, Primary Triangle Two.

The lack of conscious awareness about the nature or severity of emotional stress finds some explanation in the frequent discussions of the anatomy of the psyche and psychological mechanisms like repression, suppression, and projection, for example. These mechanisms are conferred a high degree of respect by mental health professionals and regarded as forces which operate outside the control of consciousness. The mechanisms are mostly unconscious and therefore one is powerfully subject to a law like repression. Little more than a plant that knows when to open its flower, or turn to the sun when the light is just right, the Human has unexamined mechanisms which are designed to insure its survival from a harsh emotional environment. There are ingenious means of adaptation and alteration of response in the context of new conditions, friendly or hostile.

IBFRT locates powerful emotional incoherencies like rejection, abandonment, hunger, and desire in Primary Triangle Two. Like the powerful and unexpected forces of a storm, flood, fire, or plague, the plants seem nearly powerless to survive. Yet, there is an untapped potential to adapt and perhaps even sense an upcoming catastrophe and prepare for it! Rocks apparently do not share this level of freedom. Deep in Human, there is such an activity of adaptation and survival. Imprinting reaches this layer of being with an accurate location and specific sequence to remove the damage, or loss of freedom, when a person has experienced powerful storms which only allowed the possibility of finding shelter and attending to primal survival needs. The experience of being burdened by crushing defeat of an unknown origin, or a paralyzing hopelessness that no meaningful family is achievable, or a body part is paralyzed from interacting under the conscious direction of Human are examples of the damaging effects of life's storms when the fragile Human or plant is nearing the end of its capacity to remain viable.

There is a greater degree of freedom and the belief on the part of many that not all emotional trauma is not a death sentence. PTSD has the attention of many who believe it will never fully disappear and that its sufferers will be subject to its harmful effects for the duration of life. Among this group, there is at least the admission that some treatment and limited freedom from its consequences is possible. While the contents of the second primary triangle are powerful and may become overwhelming like a violent storm, these emotional objects are a significant step closer to freedom and personal choice. Comparing it with the first primary triangle, one might describe the contents of the second primary triangle, as an infinite number of events in which the person exercised very little control over the operation of the filter.

Since the degree of flexibility to the power of emotion and lack of understanding about its origin and scope is extremely limited, this level and form of awareness is mostly unconscious. Since there is some level of response, Primary Triangle Two is reflective of a greater level of awareness than Primary Triangle One.

Primary Triangle Three.

IBFRT identifies the third primary triangle as the contextual locations for the lower mental functions, a level of mental incoherence concerning thought objects in which the perception and evaluation of these types of thoughts and processes are believed to be automatic, instinctual, or primitive. The thoughts in these contexts reflect common patterns of response and a form of programmed adaptability which includes the ability, under life threatening conditions, to leave one's roots behind and travel to a more favorable environment. Locomotion increases the range of options to insure survival. Greater decision-making power increases risk and reward. One chooses to not act upon all well-known stimuli and act decisively, in a species-specific strategy, based on the consideration of more than one option. For humans this level of awareness and response to consciously set something aside, is a form of suppression. The content of a situation is analyzed within a particular context, and a choice is made to respond accordingly. The ability to modify a nearly automatic reaction to an event is moved by another portion of consciousness to a less directly accessed location within consciousness.

Mental incoherence in the third primary triangle often is matched with stressful experiences when a painful or uncomfortable situation is avoided by changing locations or taking steps to eliminate danger or some other obstacle. These consciously chosen strategies contain an enormously large unconscious component. What is being distinguished here is the more conscious aspect of what the person is doing to survive without attempting to evaluate the wisdom of the strategy. Does a fleeing animal from a forest fire know the way to safety or only the quickest way to flee from immediate danger? The nine triangles within Primary Triangle Three indicate that not all suppressive activities have the same effect on the entire person. Introspection and insightful conversation with a trusted friend or family member may lead to the discovery of a more freely chosen and helpful response to eliminate a threat rather than to run from it or deny its existence.

While many of the thoughts that arise within us seem to be out of our control and mostly automatic, training the mind offers a different perspective. While many of the residues of suppressed thoughts and feelings seem to be stuck to us like permanent glue, there is considerable ability to free ourselves from the incoherent forces which are found in these contexts. Primary Triangle Three seems to find its freedom and lack of it under the term the *subconscious structures of awareness*. Not exactly but this level is moving in the right direction!

I would venture to say that without a miracle, there is no possibility of the power of intention affecting the physical objects. Whisperology does not exclude any object, physical or non-physical from its influence. The power to influence that aspect of Human—which is housed within the structures of the first three primary triangles—is generally perceived as limited in many instances by fixed physical laws, overwhelming trauma, or fixed patterns of animal behavior. Common collective human belief systems reinforce the perception that we have little control over these deep structures of awareness—no more than an atom of iron, a fragment of limestone, a pumpkin seed, or a frog. Common belief would say that your past is so fixed within you that these influences cannot be changed, any more than iron could decide to become copper.

Primary Triangle Four.

The contextual map of Primary Triangle Four is the entry into a higher level of awareness where there is a much greater level of control and flexibility about the collection and application of a different set of thought objects. One might say that the quality of coherence called *human coherence* is becoming more obvious.

This level of awareness is the home to many sources of consciousness which are analogously shared by some, but not all, mammalian life. I do not bring up animals to assign every creature to a particular triangular space. That is far afield from the purpose of the book. I mention other entities within the universe including animals because I want to highlight that all life—including what is regarded by most people as inanimate, unintelligent, or subhuman—is not intrinsically separate from Human. The triangles simply reflect the differing levels of shared awareness that arise from a universal consciousness (or awareness) that excludes no one or "thing." I will leave it to those who have expertise (I guess that means lots of data to support a belief system!) to decide if a dog, a squirrel, or a whale experiences conscious guilt, regret, or loneliness. Apparently, there is something about the behaviors of mammals, and perhaps other creatures, that bears the marks of courage, or the ability to adapt (the willingness to grow), and the emerging awareness which recognizes a necessary balance between all creatures which share the planet. This faint awareness is not the private revelation to Human (200 to 399 on the MOC). For my purposes, IBFRT recognizes that the quality or experience, called Awareness, is at least, in part, shared beyond the Human. Abstract reasoning and the use of the intellect to solve problems (the territory of the 400 to 499 on the MOC) is a significant new stage of development and new possibilities. Primary Triangle Four distinguishes itself because the focus of awareness has crept beyond what is required for the satiation and continuation of an isolated entity, whatever its species including Human.

The belief in the power to choose among options to accomplish a broader range of goals appears to be present because there is a considerably greater degree of freedom to consciously make decisions based on the belief that the choice may do more than insure, or attempt to insure, the preservation of individual self-interest. The limitations within these structures are somewhat appreciated by the differences between a conscious and unconscious challenge to existence, including the ability to ponder the meaning of life itself.

Primary Triangle Five.

If there is a lower consciousness structure then it must be followed by the structures of a *Higher Consciousness*. IBFRT identifies that in this region, Human surrenders its belief (at least to some extent) that science and technology have the ability to bring happiness and meaning to existence. The structures at this level of consciousness recontextualize the value of the intellect, which becomes a tool in service of a deeper purpose. There is more to life than is revealed by the best the intellect can devise. Somehow, there remains beyond the reach of the highest intellectual powers something more wondrous and glorious than any human invention. The "something more" is intuitively grasped when one watches a setting sun or listens to the organ at a Christmas Eve mass in the wee hours. What of the indescribable miracle when a child is born with the abiding presence of a parent who passed away years before? Life awakens us, intentionally and inevitably, to our purpose, and often unknown reason for incarnation into precisely chosen conditions. There are moments in which the impeccable timing of life is not unnoticed. Consider this, dear reader: What would it be to live in every moment with an awareness of a perfect timing? The first glimmers of this awareness begin in Primary Triangle Five.

The hold on what is perceived to be me, and not me, is qualitatively changed by Love. There is no doubt about it. None! There is a power in this primary triangle that constellates a coherence to an expanded level of consciousness which transforms the content of the first four primary triangles. This is the level of coherence in which healing instead of treatment, physical and spiritual, is a possibility.

Beyond individual survival, a voice within consciousness imagines a greater good in the perceived future and has the capacity to develop a planning process to accomplish a task that exceeds a personal agenda. For me, there is nothing "other-worldly", only universally resonant, about love.

All of the levels above a particular level are more powerful and influence those below it. There is a continuum of consciously, subconsciously, and unconsciously held limiting beliefs that are attached to, and amplified by, feelings. We might try to come up with a different word that best describes the consciousness and human experience of guilt, for example, for each level. However, I choose to appreciate the difference of what guilt is, and how it functions, based on the context. The context determines in what way, and to what extent, guilt exists as a limiting condition in a person's life. The content called "guilt" has a different meaning based on the level of awareness in which it influences the structure. IBFRT identifies that particular level of awareness, or mindfulness, to help the person with letting go of the guilt wherever it is located in awareness. The manifestation of the misperception of guilt, therefore, varies based on its spatial location represented by The Figure, and the overall level of consciousness.

The particular level of consciousness about a particular problem, physical or non-physical, can be very different from the overall level of consciousness. Hawkins writes, "In describing the emotional correlates of the energy fields of consciousness, it is well to remember that they rarely are manifested as pure states in an individual. Levels of consciousness are always mixed; a person may operate on one level in a given area of life and on quite another in another area. An individual's overall level of consciousness is the sum total effect of these levels."[144]

This is a crucial subject for discussion and will be emphasized repeatedly in the examples to follow. A person may have an overall level of consciousness that is kind, loving, and integrous. However, If the person's level of consciousness is calibrated about a particular problem like high blood pressure or cancer, the level of consciousness may be very different. Their responses to a crisis about health may be as limited as a plant that can't uproot itself and run from a fire, or as automatic as the response of a carnivore to its next prey, or as sterile and computer-like as the analysis of a new piece of data. On the other hand, from a higher level of consciousness which begins to emerge in Primary Triangle Five, the person who learns of the new development of a health care problem may respond from a context which expresses a spiritual truth. "The appearance of cancer is an opportunity for spiritual transformation. Not only do I accept this change in my life but I welcome the opportunity for the spiritual gifts it brings." The response to a "problem" is always a reflection of context. These differences in response are reflected in The Figure for the person which allows IBFRT to identify in what field and structure of awareness the limiting conditions exist. Yes, I just did plant another seed for Part II.

Primary Triangle Five also reflects an evolved state of consciousness in which the person is consciously connected to others, to the earth, and the universe. The level of connection is reflected in an expanded level of consciousness. The one who experiences life from this context experiences a growing awareness of deep unity, not only about what appears outside of one's personal space, but also, in some mystical

---

[144] Hawkins, *Power vs Force*, p. 60.

sense, with the entities that share the bio-body suit. There is some sentiment within me that there is a similar feeling, or belief, in Hindu theories, sometimes described as the bliss body, or cosmic consciousness. Alignment with the field of Love manifests the Highest Mind, and clarity, which surpasses the rational mind and the significant but limited powers of reason and the intellect. I believe that the comparison between The Figure and the representations within other spiritual traditions are interesting and encouraging. There is one fundamental truth and many helpful but limited positionalities, or TOEs, along the way, that are explainable based on particular historical backgrounds and cultural influences. I continue to do my own work, with God's help, knowing that there are many others who have done, or, are doing comparable spiritual activities. This is the level in which the 499 bridge is crossed, the threshold of all belief systems based on materialism, and the gateway to the primacy of love. Freedom is not regarded as the license to do anything. Freedom is a state of being characterized by love.

The apex of Primary Triangles Six and Seven point downwards symbolizing a different kind of structure, or level of coherence. The downward direction suggests levels, or realms, in which there is no separation between subject and object, a state of non-duality. In one sense, these levels of awareness are both beyond us and within us. The resources of these levels are gifts of grace from the Creator, and the source of healing. These are the timeless perceptual realms of awareness that coincide with the Hawkins MOC designation of consciousness level 600 and beyond. The point of contact of the vertex where Primary Triangle Six touches the base of The Figure is symbolized as the 600 threshold. *(See Figure 1 in the Appendix.)*

Primary Triangle Six.
If you like the word *mind* instead, I suppose you might refer to this as the lower eternal mind. The language is clearly inadequate: how

could anything eternal be lower? Silly. The structures that are symbolized here are spiritual wisdom. Wisdom suggests something far greater than intelligence or genius because the beginning of wisdom is the spiritual gift known as humility. One must surrender everything one is so proud to claim as mine, including one's own highly prized intellect to activate these structures. This primary structure is called *The Lower Spiritual Structure.*

Primary Triangle Six also designates the spaces for spiritual karma. Personal and collective spiritual karma are found within its nine triangles. Identifying the particular triangle in which personal and collective karmic incoherence are located is correlated with the lack of manifestation of a gift of the Spirit.

As it says, "in the beginning was the Word", so too, prior to any incarnation, of the Word becoming flesh, there was a governing intention. Divine Love. It is no different for human beings. The beginning occurs before conception, at the moment the choice is made to incarnate, to be a part of the physical world. This is an initial intention, a first impulse, and expression of purpose. It concludes with a final outcome that is in the physical world but the initial impulse to enter the world did not begin in it. There is a progression from the first impulse within consciousness through information structures, energetic structures, and finally physical structures. The first human impulse registers in the seventh group of triangles in the eternal aspect and miraculously in the temporal one. It encourages everyone to think that before there is any conception, every life comes into being to fulfill a purpose. The purpose is connected with the grand design of the Creator. As such, every life prior to its entry into the physical realm and space time is sacred.

Since alignment with the image and likeness of the Creator is based on purpose, not on an elusive fundamental substance, there is a renewed appreciation of Dr. William Tiller's theory and proposal of the deltron that links the temporal world with the eternal world through integrous intention. I believe that the deltron is a functional catalyst, a bridge that links the temporal and aspects together. When there is alignment with the divine intention as it is described in the commandments, or in other similar statements from other spiritual traditions, then the eternal influences the temporal aspect in ways that can only be described as healing. This also implies that it is fruitful to place the different temporal aspects of existence into different triangular spaces, not based on more fine or invisible substances, but, on the basis of intrinsic coherent intentions that are reflected in the divine purpose. Yes, there is a hierarchy— *a hierarchy of Divine Purpose.*

The themes which recur as problems in life experiences revolve around the findings in Primary Triangle Six. More will be said about this in the examples to follow in Part II.

Primary Triangle Seven

Primary Triangle Seven is called *The Higher Spiritual Structure.* For a similar reason, IBFRT prefers this designation to the more sterile sounding *higher eternal mind.* The realm is the home of the gifts of the spirit including peace, love, and joy. The spiritual gifts that manifest in time space come from here, and beyond. Healing, not treating problems, comes from and through Primary Triangles Six and Seven. The lack of alignment that manifests spiritual incoherence is the most important incoherence. Manifesting spiritual coherence is the essential purpose of human incarnation. *Increased coherence through these structures creates the most powerful influence in not only human life but the entire universe, and in every level of awareness.*

The gifts of the Spirit are expressed and accessible from every primary triangle, however, the spaces in which the gifts are correlated within The Figure are Primary Triangle Seven. *(See Figure 4 in the Appendix.)* Hierarchy of purpose and function manifests the gifts of the Spirit. The gifts of the Spirit express the divine Presence in all of creation. I believe these gifts are the foundation of the highest science and spirituality available to Human. We don't receive the gifts by earning them but by surrendering obstacles and misperceptions that are reinforced by limiting beliefs and what Hawkins calls the juice that is available when we are in love with the story of me, hero or victim.

The most important gift of the Spirit is love. The correlation is with triangle 63 and it is correlated with the elemental consciousness of oxygen. The absence of love is apathy, a level of consciousness that does not support human life.

The second gift of the Spirit is hopefulness. The correlation is with triangle 62 and it is correlated with the elemental consciousness of copper. The absence of hopefulness is despair.

The third gift of the Spirit is peacefulness. The correlation is with triangle 61 and it is correlated with the elemental consciousness of iron. The absence of peacefulness is anxiety.

The fourth gift of the Spirit is gentleness. The correlation is with triangle 60 and the element calcium. The absence of gentleness is harshness or abusiveness.

The fifth gift of the Spirit is faithfulness. The correlation is with triangle 59 and is correlated with the elemental consciousness of zinc. The absence of faithfulness is shame.

The sixth gift of the Spirit is charity, or kindness. The correlation is with triangle 58 and it is correlated with the elemental consciousness of sulfur. The absence of charity is anger.

The seventh gift of the Spirit is humility. The correlation is with triangle 57 and it is correlated with the elemental consciousness of carbon. The absence of humility is pride.

The eighth gift of the Spirit is self-control. The correlation is with triangle 56 and it is correlated with the elemental consciousness of silicon. The absence of self-control is guilt.

The ninth gift of the Spirit is joy. The correlation is with triangle 55 and it is correlated with the elemental consciousness of phosphorus. The absence of self-control is grief.

The relationship between the gifts of the Spirit and The Figure is illustrated by Figure 6. "Correlation Of Spiritual Gifts With Primary Triangle Seven" in the Appendix.

Alignment with the Eternal Aspect

The spiritual qualities of the eternal aspect are of a non-physical nature outside of space time. There is no beginning or ending. The seventh group of triangles are the most inner aspects because they contain the primary eternal principles. There is a hierarchy, but not a temporal one. Moving from the spaces in the seventh group of triangles to the first group of triangles, is a movement through a structure of principles that flow from the primary principles. In this sense they are secondary, tertiary, and so on.

While there is no temporal aspect within the eternal aspect, the opposite is not the case. There is an eternal aspect, or resonance, within every temporal aspect because it reflects an eternal intention. Alignment with the eternal aspect is based on its deepest purposes of Divine Wisdom and Divine Love which includes that the "Word became flesh." This is expressed in a symbolic way with the isosceles triangles. Instead of a "God particle," I use the triangle as a symbol that reflects the universal laws in the eternal and temporal aspects.

From the vertex emerges two vectors of equal magnitude and balancing directions. When each vector terminates, they are connected by a horizontal plane that creates the space that defines what is inside and outside of the event. Descriptions like fruits and gifts of the Spirit are connected with spaces to reflect the eternal aspect. Contrasting the temporal and eternal aspects, we see how they connect with each other through the image and likeness of the Creator. Every structure carries the same shape. Large or small, it belongs to the governing structure, recognized by its shape. The Creator creates and maintains the unity. Unity with the image and likeness of the Creator manifests coherency in heaven and on earth. Is that not what we pray for? "Thy will be done on earth as it is in heaven…"

When the governing structure is used as a tool to locate a virtual space that is incoherent for a non-temporal reason such as emotional trauma or a non-integrous way of being in the world, it will be possible to understand its manifestation in the temporal aspect. The path to alignment is not through a temporal intervention but a spiritual one. Hawkins' Map of Consciousness is one way of learning more about the governing structure. When life is not lived for an integrous purpose, the eternal aspect of the structures shows the spaces in which we are not coherent because the consciousness of the person is not coherent with the commandments. These incoherencies are manifested in the governing temporal structure.

The importance of an integrous life that creates coherence between the temporal and eternal aspects helps us appreciate the impact of an incoherent life. It is characterized by an incoherency of purpose that is deceiving, damaging, and destructive. There is a lack of love and discernment in all incoherent purposes, a significant departure from the commandments because it is small minded. It would be like a bird not knowing why it had wings. The wing of a bird, perfectly designed for flight, each component designed for flying, never being extended into the wind. So much promise of joy of soaring above the earth, using its wings to fulfill its purpose for existence. It would be like a bird choosing to hop along the ground, ignorant and disconnected from its purpose. When humans are foolish, they can be bird-brained, not applying what is knowable, in service of a goal. Grounded. Sadly, sometimes humans can be so far from their purpose that they seem to prefer it that way. I wonder, how can we possibly know what our parts were made for if we don't begin with the certainty that they were meant to fulfill a divine purpose?

We are not linked together by considering our contrasting purposes but by seeing how all purposes when aligned with how the original purpose contributes to a singular purpose. *We share a common geometry.* This is why we must be able to see within the temporal aspect of our lives the eternal aspect. This is true for an atom, a molecule, a rock, a plant, a human being, the earth, the planets, the sun, the stars, the galaxy upon galaxy, there can be no exclusions. All is created for the fulfillment of a divine purpose. It has been created and intended to manifest the eternal, spiritual laws that govern the universe. These purposes manifest Divine Love and Wisdom and are whispered into every bit of it.

The seven primary triangles describe patterns of increasing complexity and power that are expressed through the interaction between the informational networks operative in each level and the *consciousness of each person*. IBFRT identifies the use of the word *mind* as a very conscious designation for the primary triangles. Primary Triangle One would be called Physical Mind and Primary Triangle Two would be called Emotional Mind. The value of including the word *mind* is to emphasize that each level, or body, has its own mind, mindfulness, or intelligence. This is a form of consciousness, or awareness. This distinguishes mind from the brain, or a central nervous system, and reflects the belief that all of creation, including rocks, elements, and what gives the elements "life," *all participate in their own ways with universal consciousness, limiting itself by appearing in space time.* The word *intelligence* is too restrictive but still can be used to emphasize the idea that all entities are, in some sense, intelligent. This also implies that even atoms and molecules "respond" to the intentions of other forms of intelligence. This would not be possible unless there was an underlying oneness about the essential nature of all things which is hidden below, and beyond, the world of form.

This shared quality at every level is the reason why the imprinting processes of whisperology influence the body, or "subtle bodies," at the deepest level: a whisper that takes place through the interaction between the Physical Mind and the Highest Mind, that is powered by the unlimited potential of the Eternal Mind.

The same belief in a fundamental unity of all creation, beyond the separation into seven primary triangles, could be expressed by substituting the word *body* for *mind.* There is no essential difference between the two, if the intention is to express the idea that the rock, the tree, the bird, or the person, has its own "form" of self-awareness.

Usage of labels like *unconscious, subconscious,* and *conscious* structures is not a perfect answer to completely differentiate between the forms of physical, emotional, mental, karmic, and spiritual incoherence but have proven to be very helpful in the clinic.

Primary Triangles One through Five also correspond with increasing levels of complexity and autonomy in nature. IBFRT matches a particular form and level of self-awareness with different kinds of earthly entities:

Primary Triangle One, the space in which physical coherence is expressed is the realm of awareness shared by atoms, molecules, rocks, bacteria, blood cells, and brains.

Primary Triangle Two, the space in which emotional coherence is expressed is the realm of awareness of algae, yeast, oak trees, and rose bushes.

Primary Triangle Three, the space in which lower mental coherence is expressed is the realm of awareness of fish, frogs, snakes, and birds.

Primary Triangle Four, the space in which higher mental coherence is expressed is the realm of mammals.

Primary Triangle Five, the space in which human coherence is expressed is the realm of Human. Each primary triangle group reflects its own forms of intelligence and ability to interact with its internal and external environment.

Through the power of intention, humans are given the capacity to coherently align with all of these spaces. Through the power of intention, humans are also given the capacity to be aligned to the spaces within Primary Triangle Six and Primary Triangle Seven, to complete deep spiritual purposes. This requires the letting go of misperceptions about survival and happiness with the world based on the acquisition of external objects to protect us and make us feel whole.

The laws which are operative in space time regarding the material world, whether it be a piece of granite, a bacterium, or striated muscle, are the same and well described by the positionalities of the "hard sciences" and are mostly predictable (that is, unless you are familiar with chaos theory and non-linear dynamics). The key point that is being made here is that different levels of awareness operate within different physical structures but the level of awareness that is closest to the material world, appears to operate mostly according to the laws of chemistry. What are described by most people as miracles, or a spontaneous healing, is a powerful example, that the highest levels of awareness may transform that which is perceived to be inert, without consciousness, or separate from higher levels of consciousness.

All of the spaces and levels of awareness are connected and interactive. The spaces are abstractions in time space for elements which are fundamentally and infinitely one. Exploring the spaces at different time points in the test subject's life is, from an expanded level of consciousness, is also an abstraction of that which is eternally one. Accessing the primary layers below or beyond, and their elemental qualities is to differentiate that when all positionalities are transcended, is also complete *in itself*. These might be considered as archetypal and elemental, the space in which it arises within awareness, and the numerical sequences which navigate into a new positionality and context.

There will be a primary space and level of awareness that expresses the overall positionality of the subject, which is referred to as the *overall triangle coherence*. The location of the overall triangle coherence is a useful starting point from which to measure the change in consciousness that occurs through whisperology.

CHAPTER SIX
THE FIRST USE OF THE TOOL

Different uses of the tool are based on what are considered to be different aspects of the design and composition of the tool. New applications of the tool also come through the experience of using the tool which alters the positionality of its user with respect to The Figure. In other words, the context of the user of The Figure cannot be separated from the understanding of how the tool is used to treat a variety of troubles in the "house" called Human.

How the tool is applied is dependent on the positionality of its user.

There are two primary orientations, or positionalities. The first use of the tool begins in the physical world because the application *appears* to reflect the linear belief system that many health problems have a physical cause. There *appears* to be a simple chain of events, a "cause and effect" scenario, through which Physical Cause A produced Physical Problem B which produced Physical Cause C that eventually led to Physical Problem D and so on. The common-sense sounding approach is to find the part that is not working properly and fix it, not unlike a car that needs a new alternator or muffler. Physical experiences, including unpleasant symptoms and a lack of physical well-being, are assumed to be the result of a physical problem.

The first use of The Figure only appears to resemble the positionality of conventional medicine and orthodox thinking which *believes* in the primacy and reality of a physical, material world. However, *the paradigm of causality is transcended by whisperology and its tools.*

Why? Because only the manifestation of physical incoherence, not its origin, is in the physical world. From a particular level of consciousness which is expressed in The Figure, the linear arises from the non-linear. The linear is an expression of its non-linear origin. From the consciousness level of science which reaches its apex at 499, the first use of the tool does not make sense and is impossible. From a non-linear context beyond 499, the first use of the tool not only makes sense, it works! Even if the tool is used to explore and eliminate physical incoherence, the application is based on a level of consciousness which believes that physical incoherence is a manifestation of limiting conditions that originate within the non-linear realm of consciousness not the material world. *Physical incoherence is eliminated by healing the non-linear, not by treating the physical.*

Hawkins points out the enormous obstacle that is often insurmountable when two paradigms collide. He writes, "the confusion surrounding the nature of truth can be mitigated if we calibrate the level of truth of our questions as well as our answers. Paradoxes and ambiguities arise from confusing levels of consciousness; an answer is true only at its own level of consciousness. Thus. We may find that an answer is 'correct' but simultaneously 'invalid,' like a musical note that is correctly played at the wrong place in the score."[145]

The collision between the two different forms of consciousness is based on the failure to recognize that the significance and meaning of any content including what is perceived to be physical, real, and repeatable is always based on context. This collision is a common experience

---

[145] Ibid, p. 90

in the clinic because the contextual field of most patients about their health is the conventional medical model. The examples to follow will help to illustrate the confusion of levels of consciousness and offer an expanded context that has been helpful to many.

The answers patients seek to their problems are limited by the questions. Sometimes the best one can do is to invite someone to consider a problem differently than he or she has done so in the past. I have seen the healing power that comes when new questions lead to a contextual shift. Hawkins encourages self-exploration beyond what we have been told to believe about ourselves including our health. He writes, "We discover the truth about ourselves because our questions themselves are merely the reflections of our own motives, goals and levels of awareness. It is always informative to calibrate not the answer, but the question."[146]

While we may begin the exploration of a physical problem by considering physical incoherence, in whisperology, our questions will locate the physical experiences *within a spiritual framework*. What appeared to be a physical, objective problem confirmed by an objective test appears to lead inevitably to a non-physical, incoherent condition. Standardized lab tests will not tell you that there is a deeper understanding of the physical outcome beyond the test itself that is contained but hidden from the assumptions of the test within a non-physical state. There are no measures, by definition, in the conventional world to identify it, much less put into a report. At best, anomalies may appear that are attributed in a limited paradigm to laboratory error and the conclusion that the test should be repeated. A repeated lab test is designed to refute questions about its accuracy, not its significance, or its ability to answer a deeper question.

If we are focused on the physical side of the fence, IBFRT will locate a *primary contextual space* within the first primary triangle *but it*

---

[146] Ibid, p. 94

is not the only affected space. Other spaces are affected because the actualization of multiple physical potentials that emerge, arise from related but distinct contexts. For example, the incoherence in a particular tendon is reflected in the incoherent blood supply to a nearby structure. The two structures, the tendon and the blood vessel, are not causally linked but their contexts (and rules of governance that establish the content within the related spaces) are similar enough that there is a blended relationship or overlapping of the two contexts. Secondly, since all of the spaces are connected with one another because they are integral to The Figure, any change in the content of a particular contextual space affects the other spaces, *but not all of the spaces to the same degree.* The elephant in the room, in this example about blood supply, are the non-physical conditions between blood flow and other forms of incoherence, like fear or anger. Identification of the correct primary contextual space reveals other relationships besides those within the first primary triangle. If you think about it, this makes sense because of the obvious connections between the physical body and the structures of awareness which govern the rest of our being and experiencing.

Another way of stating the indissoluble connection between the physical and the spiritual, is to intuitively realize that beyond the surface of human experience, *the physical is contained within the non-physical.* The power of The Figure is appreciated because it expresses, albeit imperfectly, the inseparability of the physical from the non-physical and correspondence of human experience with all levels of creation. The two inner primary triangles point downward into creation, surrounded by the five outer primary triangles which point upward toward the Source of existence. The Figure also symbolizes the unity of subject and object. We "relate" to The Figure as if it were an object but each one of us *is in The Figure*, because as a subject, each person is positioned within a particular space, as part of the whole and as one.

The correspondences between the primary triangle and a "house" problem express the truth that incoherent conditions manifest misperception in all levels of being. Even if attention is directed to what appears to be only a physical issue, or problem, The Figure recontextualizes what is perceived to be physical as a superficial understanding of what is wrong. The core of the problem lies within the non-physical foundation of the house. Alternatively, if the second application governs the use of The Figure, to explore, for example, an emotional or spiritual problem like anxiety or addiction, the manifestations of these struggles will also be obvious in the physical body. While mainstream medicine is quick to label many psychological struggles and experiences as diseases, it is reluctant to consider physical problems and diseases like cancer as having their origins in consciousness.

The first use of the tool begins with the assumption that the problem to explore is of a physical nature and some event(s) that take place within space time. Let's consider two examples of how the first use of the tool is applied to different situations. *<u>Any names which refer to a person in these examples are completely fictitious.</u>*

To gain a better sense of how the interaction with patients takes place, the thought processes of how The Figure is used, and when the imprinting is being done, I will present the examples for the first application of the tool in an informal conversational style. The feedback from readers was that describing the new methods through a series of exchanges with my imaginary friend Morgan made the book easier to understand and more enjoyable.

Example One. Physical Trauma

Maggie, a middle-aged woman experiencing problems with her back, hips, and legs sought relief from stiffness and pain that was only somewhat, and temporarily, relieved by medication and manual therapies. I asked her if she had ever injured her hip. Maggie told me that six years earlier, she injured her hip when she fell on an ice-covered sidewalk. When I asked her if there had been any other physical traumas, she told me about two car accidents: one that happened a few years prior to the fall, and an earlier car accident that happened when she was in college. I wrote down the approximate times of the car accidents and the fall. I also asked Maggie if she had "all of her parts." Surgery leaves surgical traumas, too, like the removal of the gallbladder, or a hysterectomy, even if these events took place many years ago. Maggie told me that her twenty-nine-year-old son was a Caesarian birth and that she had hernia surgery two years ago. I wrote down the known times of the birth and the hernia surgery. Most patients are very willing to share this information. What people usually don't realize is that physical trauma, accidental or surgical, is an aspect of physical incoherence. I refer to these as limiting conditions. The conversation, whisperology testing, and treatment go something like this:

Steve: There are lots of things that affect the pain in your back, hips, and legs. Old injuries, surgeries… your body doesn't forget. The accidents and surgeries leave their marks in your body, even if they happened a long time ago. I am going to do some things to find how it is stored in your body, and then, do something I call imprinting to send all of the trauma away.

Maggie: I don't understand what you mean or how you're going to do that…

Steve: It's hard to explain. I've come up with a couple of analogies that I think will help this make some sense. Think of a house. A house is made up of materials like bricks, wood, shingles, and so on. But you don't have a house unless you've got a construction crew with the right tools and skills to build the house. Right? And, you could have the best raw materials, the best crew with the best tools, but they can only build what is in the plans, the blueprint. In a way, your body, all the cells, organs, and tissues, are like the materials of the house. It's what you see. All of the processes going on inside of you, some which can be studied by medicine, and others which are invisible to conventional science, but detectable through other systems, like acupuncture and Chinese medicine, are like the construction crew, which keeps using its tools and expertise to replace old cells with new ones, or give the body what it needs to function. Sometimes I refer to what I do as "information-based medicine" because I go upstream, as far as I can, to look for problems with the plans. Imprinting restores the plans that are used which eventually manifest in the creation of your body parts. Does that help?

Maggie: I sort of get what you mean…

Steve: Another way of saying it would be something like this. Let's say that you're on your computer. You open up an email from someone you don't know and all of a sudden, your computer has a virus. If the virus is really nasty, then your computer software might be badly damaged so that it stops working. Or, maybe, it just slows it down, and doesn't work as well as it used to. The software called Maggie, the informational programs that determine how you work, can be affected by physical trauma, just like what happens when you get a virus on your computer.

Maggie: That's very interesting. I never thought of it like that…

Steve: What I'm going to do is use my tools to locate these traumas. Then, I'm going to use my mind to imprint information to remove these "viruses from your software". This will take me a few minutes to figure out and do the imprinting. Before I do that, it might be kind of fun to do a couple of things so that you can better feel what is going on…

Let me hold onto your right leg at your ankle. I'm going to move it laterally, very slowly, away from your body. Tell me when you first feel any tightness. I don't care if you feel it in your back, your hip, your groin, your thigh, your knee—it doesn't matter where. This is not to see how far I can stretch you until you say "uncle," but to find the point where the resistance begins.

Maggie: OK

(I move her leg and she felt the resistance in her groin area after moving her leg laterally by approximately forty-five degrees. I returned her leg to the original position.)

Steve: Was that OK?

Maggie: Yes

Steve: Now I want you to tell me what your pain is like right now. How bad is it? Show me what movement makes the pain worse.

Maggie: Well, I feel the pain now but it's worse if I sit for a long time. Actually, I feel it no matter what I do. Lying down, sitting, walking...

Steve: OK. Well, I'm ready to get started. Let's see what happens.

(With my hands gently holding on to Maggie's ankles, I silently identify where to begin by using IBFRT. The best place to begin is identified when the intention is truthful and useful.)

In other books, I described the initial steps that must be taken prior to the specifics of Maggie's problem. In every instance, it is imperative to begin the testing by asking if there is permission to test the person. I also believe that it is essential to hold in mind the intention to honor all that God is manifesting through this person in the testing process. I will not include this portion of the preparation in the examples. *Know that it is the starting point of every test and treatment.*

The place to begin the process will vary so it is important to assume that the order of imprinting does not always appear in chronological order. In this instance, I am to begin with the car accidents—first the college accident and then the one that took place a few years ago. IBFRT identifies the location of the event of the first accident in Primary Triangle One, Triangle 2. Many physical traumas are located in Triangle 2 but not all of them.

The primary triangle that I ask "to be taken to" includes the event. Then I ask for the specific triangle within the group. Finally, I divide the triangle into seven sub-triangles. This division could continue with each division triangulating the event in a smaller space. However, it has not been necessary to magnify the area beyond the division of one of the 63 elements into seven sections. This expands the entire map to 441 sub-triangles. *(See Figure 7. "Maggie's Test" in the Appendix. The illustration only shows the parts of The Figure that are relevant to her test.)*

Once the sub-triangle is found, the coherence of the sub-triangle is determined. Prior to the event, the coherence of the space within the sub-triangle is relatively high, but after the injury the coherence is significantly lower. The coherence levels are determined by the IBFRT method. A sequence is developed to restore the coherence of the area. The sequence is imprinted through intention with the hands on the person's ankles. After the imprinting process is completed, the coherence of the area is reevaluated. The area described by the sub-triangle, is now 100 percent, or nearly 100 percent coherent.)

Steve: I'm going to start with eliminating the stress from the first car accident and then do the same for the second accident.

Maggie: OK

(The sub-triangle is found in Triangle 2 and level of coherence determined. *(See Figure 7. "Maggie's Test" in the Appendix.)* Usually, I will call to mind a few indicators before determining the sequence. For physical trauma, good examples of indicators are atlas, cranial bones, head and neck trauma, pain, blood pressure, and anxiety. There are plenty of others that could be used. I sometimes write them down and a numerical value for the incoherence of every chosen indicator to assess the outcome after imprinting. The sequence in this case was 372 717 675 797. How the sequence is imprinted through the hands into the patient and what is held in mind during the imprinting process was described in the second book of this series.

After the imprinting of the sequence is completed, I talk briefly with Maggie.)

Steve: How was that? Was that OK?

Maggie: I'm not sure what you just did but I felt my whole body relax. That's amazing!

Steve: I'm just getting started. The relaxation is your body, actually your whole person, letting you know that it feels good to eliminate the stress of the first accident. Time to imprint for the second accident.

(A different sub-triangle is found in Triangle 2 for the second car accident. (*See Figure 7. "Maggie's Test" in the Appendix.*) The sequence for this accident was 382 818 685 898. The numbers that comprise the sequence are very similar but reflect a completely different event and sub-triangle. The sequence is imprinted.)

Steve: Are you doing OK?

Maggie: Feeling better still.

Steve: Good. It's time to address the fall and the surgeries.

(At this point, I may mentally recheck indicators. Typically, some or, all of them are much less incoherent. I also may have rechecked the movement of the lateral leg but there is no hurry. This can wait until all of the physical trauma sequences are identified and imprinted. IBFRT indicates that the incoherence introduced by the C-section needs to be treated next. The location is found in the sixth triangle of Primary Triangle One. The sub-triangle is located, the level of coherence determined, and the sequence is determined. The sequence was 287 818 988 838.)

Steve: I'm treating the stress from your C-section next. Here we go…

(After the imprinting was completed, I checked in with Maggie.)

Steve: Was that OK?

Maggie: My entire abdomen relaxed. I didn't know how much stress I was carrying.

(While she is answering my question, I am listening *with my hands*. The peacefulness in my hands tells me that she is expressing exactly how she feels.)

Steve: Let's get to the rest of it. Next is the imprinting for the hernia surgery...

(A second sub-triangle is located in Triangle 6. After determining the level of coherence, the sequence 469 616 763 696 is generated, and imprinted.)

Steve: Feel good?

Maggie: Yes... hard to believe... you haven't given me anything.

Steve: And now the trauma from the fall on the ice...

(A sub-triangle in the first triangle of Primary Triangle One is the correct location. The same steps are followed to generate the sequence 374 757 779 717. This completes the list of identified physical traumas identified by the patient and deemed to be significant contributors to Maggie's local conditions. If I had not done so already, this would be the time I would check, or recheck, the chosen indicators. This would include the indicators that I recorded on paper, or just mentally filed away, and the lateral movement of her right leg.)

Steve: Well that takes care of the imprinting. Let's check the leg movement. Do you have any pain?

Maggie: No pain at all lying down.

(I repeat the lateral leg test. There is no resistance to the lateral leg movement until the leg has been moved over ninety degrees, more than twice the original distance. I have observed the astonished looks of patients and the family members or friends who often accompany the patient during the testing and treatment. The experience is magical.)

Maggie: Oh, my God. I can't believe it! How is that possible?

Steve: We better stop or you'll be ready for the circus.

Additional comments about Example One

Figure 7. "Maggie's Test" illustrates the steps that were taken to help Maggie. This is a typical example when physical trauma from accidents or surgeries are limiting conditions. Removing the informational structures from these traumas allows the body to do what it intended to do. Heal. Recover. Return to the performance of those tasks for which it was created in the first place.

In this example, the pain in the back, hips, and legs was almost completely eliminated. In many cases, the pain is completely gone. Of course, there are many instances in which other limiting conditions are relevant in order to complete resolution of a problem. Examples that are connected to other types of limiting conditions will be shared in other examples.

There are other interesting aspects to identifying and treating physical trauma that have proven useful. Let me explain by using the example of Maggie. Maggie identified five events that are classified as Physical Trauma by IBFRT. But could there be more traumas that she doesn't remember? The answer is yes, absolutely. If the H vial for Physical Trauma still tests for incoherence then there are obviously other physical traumas. How are these traumas identified, located within The Figure, and treated? The answer to these questions is to use IBFRT to match the H vial for Physical Trauma to a time period. Once the time period is identified—and there could be several periods—Maggie can be asked if she recalls any incidents from the time period. Sometimes this will trigger a memory. The same process is used to clear the triggered events. However, perhaps Maggie has no recollection of any event associated with the time period. The time period may be incorrect or she simply doesn't remember. Hold the physical trauma in mind and use IBFRT to locate the triangle, and, if it tests to be helpful, the sub-triangle. Again, all of these types of events will be found somewhere within Primary Triangle One.

The coherence of the area is determined prior to the time period when the "problem" manifested itself, and the loss of coherence in the selected year of the traumatic event. The sequence to create coherence is identified by IBFRT and imprinted. The process continues by repeating the initial question to find another time location. Prior to the repetition of the process, it is essential to ask if there is permission to continue.

The answer can be no. I understand this to mean that there is a limit to the amount of information that can be imprinted at any particular time. On the average, most people can receive this form of imprinting from one to five times in a single session.

Example Two. Iatrogenic Effects

Ted has come to the clinic for relief of arthritis symptoms. His primary complaint is sore and stiff joints, especially his left knee. A total knee replacement did not fix the knee problem but actually made matters worse. He has difficulty opening and closing his very large and weathered hands. Ted is retired but farmed all of his life. Ted's other complaints included acid reflux and high blood pressure for which he took prescription medications to treat the symptoms. He experienced some relief of his joint pain by taking over-the-counter medicines like Tylenol and ibuprofen.

The focus of this example is the contribution of iatrogenic effects to Ted's current condition; however, I would also be asking similar questions to those posed to Maggie about past injuries and physical trauma. Obviously, treatment would include removing the trauma from the knee replacement. These aspects of the testing and treatment are not discussed in this example. The same type of approach is used with all of my patients about how to explain what I am doing through the testing and imprinting process, so I will not repeat these parts of the discussion with Ted. Only that part of the conversation which is relevant to iatrogenic effects is shared in Example Two.

Steve: What medications are you taking?

Ted: I take a blood pressure pill, a Prilosec, a baby aspirin, and ibuprofen… sometimes Tylenol, and antihistamines during ragweed season.

Steve: How are you feeling now?

Ted: Stiff… especially in the morning. Lotta' phlegm when I get up. I feel a little better after I start moving around but my knee is the worst. Hard to get up if I sit too long.

(My hands are on Ted's ankles while he answers my questions. In my mind, I am attentive to the side effects of medications. I sense the level of stress introduced into his system from the medications. I know that even though the medications may help Ted to manage some of his symptoms, there are unwelcome side effects which accompany all of them. The side effects to medications, including antibiotics and vaccines, are always located in Primary Triangle One. For an unknown reason, it is necessary to imprint separately for vaccines, antibiotics, and medications. In addition to the iatrogenic effects of the medications, there is stress from x-rays and titanium with his knee replacement. I use IBFRT to tell me *in what order the stresses should be treated*, and, as I previously mentioned, when to treat the iatrogenic effects would be placed within the broader context of physical trauma. Most, but not all of the time, IBFRT indicates that the traumas from injuries and surgeries should be treated first.)

Steve: I am going to imprint some information into your system through my hands to get rid of side effects from the medications. Before I do that, I want to get an idea of the stiffness in your left knee. Show me how much it bends and at what point the pain gets worse.

(Ted bends his knee only slightly before telling me that the pain increases.)

Ted: That's as far as it goes.

(I imprint in four different locations. Two sub-triangles in triangle 1, one sub-triangle in triangle 2, and a very small sub-triangle in triangle 6. There is an interesting observation to share about the imprinting in triangle 6 because it is an example of the "triangles within triangles" method. In this example, only the incoherence related to incompatibility with titanium required a smaller space to be identified. The multiplication of triangles, if applied to the entire Figure, would be 250,047 tiny triangles! Triangle 6 was partitioned into 3969 triangles before IBFRT indicated no further subdivisions were required. *See Figure 8. "Ted's Test" in the Appendix.)*

Steve: Let's try the knee again. I'm guessing you feel more relaxed...

Ted: Like I could take a nap.

Ted bends his knee but this time there is no pain and there is an increase in the range of motion of about thirty degrees.

Ted: How did you do that? No pain and I can bend it...

Steve: Your body was affected by the medications that you are taking as well as the titanium... the imprinting has removed a lot of the stress...

Ted: For good? Permanently?

Steve: I don't know. What I would like you to do is to reinforce the imprinting by reimprinting the same information with some numerical sequences. We want your body to become permanently compatible with the titanium and that may take some time. For the medications you are currently taking, I will give you a sequence to read ten times in a row, twice a day, to prevent the reintroduction of side effects that also affect your knee. It doesn't matter if you read them out loud or silently because it is your intention and the specificity of the sequence that is required for the sequence to work.

Ted: I don't get how this works. How long do I have to do the numbers?

Steve: For the titanium side effects, at least a month. I think that you will need the other sequence for the current medications, prescription and over-the-counter, for as long as you are taking them.

Additional Comments About Example Two

Creating sub-triangles is a common activity with the first use of the tool.

A potential source of confusion about this example is the location of a titanium incoherence in Primary Triangle One, Triangle 6. The *context* of the test was to improve the function of his knee. This led to a specific space within Triangle 6 that was useful to help Ted recover more fully from his surgery. If you compare the location for helping solve Ted's "titanium-related knee replacement problem" with "elemental coherence" there is a vastly different location. Figure 5. "Correlation Of The Elements With The Figure" shows that titanium is correlated in Primary Triangle Five, Triangle 37. How is the difference explained? The answer is that the *context of the question*, "what will help Ted's titanium-related knee replacement?" is entirely different from "what space in The Figure correlates with the spiritual element titanium?" The Figure is a contextual map. Imprinting, and always with permission, to treat elemental incoherence creates coherencies beyond the physical plane.

In Ted's case, there would have been a minor reduction of elemental incoherence regarding titanium by treating his knee problem. Why not treat him for elemental incoherence by focusing attention on Triangle 37? The answer is simple but perhaps unsatisfying or confusing to the reader. IBFRT followed the questions that arose from Ted's desire and my willingness to help him with his stiffness, including his knee. There was permission to help him in this specific way. Hypothetically, if IBFRT showed that elemental coherence could be treated, then Triangle 37 might have been the answer. My experience with elemental coherence testing is that often other elements are identified than what one might think *because the context of the testing is different.* Using elemental coherence methods is an immensely powerful tool that is beyond the scope of this example of the *first* use of the tool. Training others to use The Figure frequently triggers these kinds of questions. The answers always come back to the context of the question and the specificity of the target of intention. This subject is also important in the generation of numerical sequences which was a key topic in *Intention Based Field Resonance Testing: The Magnification of the Whisper*.

A second point of discussion about this example is the importance of finding ways to help Ted to relate to a form of therapy that is completely foreign to his experience. In this example, l try to give Ted an idea about why the numbers are helpful. This topic was previously discussed in the exchanges with my imaginary friend Morgan so you might find it helpful to read that book. With Ted, one approach I often use is something like this:

Ted: Can you tell me more about the numbers?

Steve: The numbers convert an intention about a target into a language that your body understands. It's not just the body itself but the larger part of you that contains all the information about how your body is designed to do what it needs to do including your knee.

(I point to a picture on the wall.)

Steve: See that picture over there? We both agree we are looking at the same thing. We might even use some of the same words to describe it but we don't perceive it in exactly the same way. Why? Because we are different people and what things, like that picture, mean to us, what we see, and how we feel about what we are looking at, will always be different. For me to help you with your knee, we need to eliminate the perceptual differences between us about the troubles with your knee... what you feel when you walk on it, what you think is wrong with it, your beliefs about what will happen to your knee in the future... How do we do that? The sequences I am giving you today are fifteen digits long. That's fifteen degrees of freedom... fifteen variables that ensure what I am intending about getting rid of the side effects of the titanium will mean the same thing to the larger part of you that knows this language of numerical sequences. The sequence makes sure that the picture of titanium side effects is the same for both of us. When you repeat the sequence that I am giving you, you are repeating the same intention that has removed the pain from your knee and helped it to move more freely. The sequence is like a foreign language to you, just a bunch of numbers, but to your consciousness, it is a language understood by all human beings.

(This approach has been helpful to many people who have wondered why the numerical sequences are effective. I have come to believe that the numerical sequences are the most powerful delivery system of healing intention in the whisperology toolbox.)

CHAPTER SEVEN
The Second use of the Tool

Regardless of appearances, the second use of the tool begins with consideration of the non-physical incoherencies. This use of the tool does not negate the physical appearance or aspect of a problem but begins with a larger context, an expanded frame of reference. For example, if there is a chronic physical problem, there will be an emotional and mental context which recontextualizes the illness, believing that it originated within a non-physical domain. If the karmic components are included then it is further recontextualized and is not perceived to be an accident at all, but a meaningful development. The unforeseen misfortune is not a random occurrence. An originating influence within consciousness unfolded according to incoherent, or limiting, conditions that reflects the level of spiritual health, as well as individual and collective karmic patterns.

The spiritual approach culminates with a powerful life-changing realization that may become integral to the consciousness of the patient and affect his or her health in all aspects including the body. Since for most people, the most powerful fear around illness is cancer, I will illustrate what I mean by using cancer as an example. There is the possibility to achieve a level of consciousness and positionality about cancer which does not respond to the dreaded illness as a curse or cruel fate, but as an unexpected blessing and communication from the Great Unseen: *To be aware that cancer is an invitation and opportunity for spiritual transformation, and, therefore, love the cancer, for the gift it brings.* I describe this state as *cancer coherence*. You can substitute any disease, affliction, accident, or tragedy, for the word *cancer* and you have the most important homework to do in the classroom of earthly life. It is not within the scope of any lab test or medical exam to provide the person with this silver lining, however, The Figure appears to capture some aspect of this transformative context by identifying it as karmic and spiritual coherence.

These concepts are thoroughly described in Hawkins' books *Healing and Recovery*, and *Letting Go*, two invaluable resources that I have suggested to many of my patients. Hawkins encourages the spiritual seeker to uncover any illusions that are being held in consciousness like thoughts, feelings, positionalities, and fears which constitute the soil in which cancer, or any other illness, takes root and grows. For example, he emphasizes the power of unconscious guilt in all cancers. His ideas and experiences have been essential in the development of my understanding of the relationship between the physical and non-physical aspects of every disease. Many new additional H vials were created (I call them H vials in honor and recognition of his work) to differentiate and explore the locations in The Figure of different kinds of emotions, thoughts, feelings, moods, and fears. The locations of unconscious guilt compared to conscious guilt are very different. Fear of losing your home has a very different location within The Figure than worrying about your level of accomplishment and the fear of being, or not being, successful.

The second use of the tool appears to place the emphasis on function over substance. The creation, at every level, is organized according to the way in which an individual purpose is joined coherently with other individual purposes for a collective purpose. Every aspect of the creation bears the image and likeness of the Creator *only when it is accomplishing the purpose for which it was created.* This is true for every level of purpose. All of the "bodies" which comprise Human are manifested for a specific intention.

For example, the tendons of the hand carry the image and likeness of the Creator when these structures are completely coherent. The tendons are completely coherent *only when the purpose of the wrist is completely coherent.* The wrist is completely coherent only when the purpose that governs its movement is completely coherent. The thought process moves us into a hierarchy of purpose that eventually brings us to the originating purpose for the person to have a link between the hand and the arm.

The primary task is the alignment of purpose at every level of organization so that we manifest the image and likeness of the Creator.

In this application, the focus is not on a divine substance or state. The 63 elements are not magical substances or energies. Furthermore, humans are not composed of the 63 elements. *Humans are connected with the 63 elements when the purpose for a temporal aspect of a life is aligned with the original, complete, perfect, and eternal purpose that created the temporal aspect.* The Figure may be likened to a prism. In the medium of Human, the light of creation is refracted into 63 spiritual elements. The 63 spiritual elements manifest seven bodies with nine spiritual elements governing each body. The prism, as an analogy for The Figure, is 9.9 out of 10.

The second use of the tool connects purpose with the primacy of the gifts of the Spirit.

IBFRT demonstrates the correlations between particular health conditions and the lack of coherence with the gifts of the Spirit. The second use of the tool identifies spaces within The Figure to restore emotional, mental, spiritual, and karmic coherence. IBFRT is used to identify the seven primary triangles, and the 63 individual triangles, to locate the space in which the originating purpose and power of the gifts of the Spirit are correlated. Healing takes place when misperceptions are surrendered so that there is alignment within consciousness to the gifts of the Spirit and the restoration of integrous purpose at every level, in each of the seven primary triangles, or "bodies."

The second use of the tool is also compatible with seeing The Figure as a map of individual and collective karmic patterns. The Figure is used to correlate karmic incoherencies with the spiritual incoherencies, thereby providing insight about the challenges in the present life due to a lack of coherence with particular gifts of the Spirit. Until the underlying spiritual incoherence within consciousness is identified, the person will continue to be signed up for the same class on earth, revisiting the same issues, experiences, and misfortunes ("accidents") in an endless variety of forms. The Figure is a way of appreciating a truth that is nearly impossible to accept in our lives. There are no accidents.

David Hawkins responded to the experience of a miraculous healing and its relationship to karma in the following way:

"Q: What of the 'miraculous'?"

"A: If the karma of the visitor is 'ripe' and merely needs the catalyst of a higher energy to manifest, then such a potentiality may actualize. It is neither intended nor willed by the sage but happens spontaneously. Often, even the sage does not realize it has happened until witnesses report it. It is not viewed as special any more than an apple falling off a tree. It is seen as the natural course of events as they unfold in the manifest world.

Healings take place of their own accord, and in a true healing, whether the affliction disappears or not is relatively immaterial because the actual healing occurs from within. Consciousness is a state of knowing that transcends the physical. What is often relieved is not necessarily the physical or mental affliction but the suffering that has accompanied it. The miracle occurs as a transformation of context. The actual 'event' is within consciousness itself, and thus, the transformation of the afflicted person's consciousness brings about a self-healing which may or may not be exhibited externally."[147]

Hawkins described the relationship between misperception and suffering, "that which is the Infinite Presence is always present and its realization occurs of itself when the obstacles to that realization are removed. It is therefore not necessary to study the truth but only to let go of that which is fallacious. Moving away the clouds does not cause the sun to shine but merely reveals that which was hidden all along."[148]

Health and expression of purpose is birthed through an intention that begins with the Creator in the realm of unlimited potential. The fulfillment of the potential connects with every structure, every time period and beyond, every level of organization, and every sphere of the universe. The tool expresses the truth that all forms of life are connected to each other through the 63 elements (spaces). For the human being, it is a tool that may be used to restore what has been lost, damaged, or destroyed by realignment of the temporal with the eternal.

IBFRT uses The Figure to uncover karmic incoherence. When the triangles are located and reflect this form of incoherence, the connection with the particular "clouds" of misperception that obscure a spiritual gift are revealed. A person may be subject to a cycle in which the overall weather pattern does not change because attention is focused on what is taking place outside the human house, not within it. When attention is focused on the weather pattern as a series of external events, sometimes welcomed but sometimes ominous, the security of the house fluctuates from day to day. There can be no safety by harboring the illusion that one is at the mercy of the capriciousness and unpredictability of the looming clouds. The owner of the house finds it nearly impossible to

---

[147] Hawkins, *I: Reality and Subjectivity*, p. 362.
[148] Hawkins, *The Eye of the I*, p. 117.

fathom that he or she is summoning the very weather patterns that engender fear.

Let us continue to compare a person to a homeowner. The house is not only a place of shelter and comfort because he believes that he owns it. It is his. He protects it. He admires it. He sees it as a reflection of his success. Sometimes he worries about losing it. The homeowner makes every effort to manage the anxiety of losing his house by attempting to control and contain any damage from an unexpected change in the weather pattern. Every cloud may bring a threatening storm. The fear is addressed through a strategy to prevent any breach of the exterior of the house. The homeowner dreams about the moment when every situation has been anticipated and managed so that he cannot lose his home. He tries to convince himself that all is well, as long as everything "out there" is under control. Sadly, trying to control the events of the human experience is not peaceful and certainly not to be equated with spiritual peace. When the home is filled with peace, there is nothing in any weather pattern that can destroy it. In such a state of awareness, the clouds become less dark and ominous, eventually evaporating into nothingness. The homeowner eventually realizes the paradoxical truth that the illusion of control promises only the certainty of even more powerful storms and clouds. There is nothing peaceful about this realization until the fear and urge to control has been completely surrendered. No longer does the homeowner listen to the ego which has instilled the belief that to surrender fear and hypervigilance would be to invite disaster. When the homeowner stops listening to the ego and its endless meteorological forecasts, the storms vanish.

Regardless of the type of storm clouds (anxiety, anger, grief, hopelessness, arrogance, etc.) that appear to threaten the homeowner, the karmic opportunity to transcend the situation through inner spiritual transformation and alignment with the eternal sunlight is the same.

The following example illustrates that healing comes from through the evolution of consciousness. The physical body is a benefactor of this process not the cause. This case is shared with the permission of the patient but the name is withheld to honor privacy.

Example Three. A Life Changing Accident

More than ten years ago, a man came to see me for a shoulder problem. He tried many forms of treatment that were not successful. I treated him using some of the methods described in my first book and he enjoyed a complete recovery.

I did not hear from him for several years until March of 2019, when he contacted the clinic. He had relocated to Florida, and in January of 2018, he fell and suffered a severe fracture of his left ankle. Over the course of about a year, he had four surgeries which included the insertion of a plate and screws (removed in the second surgery), and the insertion of bags of antibiotics into the ankle to rid the area of infection. He received many drugs including pain killers, steroids, and oral as well as intravenous antibiotics. After the fourth surgery, he was told that his foot required amputation. After the announcement he called Ardith to ask if I might see him.

He flew up to Wisconsin and stayed in the hotel adjacent to the clinic for one week. He was scheduled for three appointments during the week. I especially remember the first visit on Friday. He came into the clinic using a scooter because it was too painful to bear any weight on his left leg. With difficulty, I helped him get up onto the testing table. For the next ninety minutes, I imprinted to remove the traumas and iatrogenic effects of the cadre of medications. Triangles were identified and sequences were imprinted to remove the trauma of four surgeries and the fall itself. The same process was used to remove the side effects of antibiotics, steroids, and pain medications.

These steps were necessary for his recovery, but the most important aspect of the testing on Friday was the calibration of his level of consciousness, including the positionality about the accident. The triangle that reflected his positionality about the fall was anger. His overall level of consciousness was in the upper 190's (Primary Triangle 3), a common finding for someone who is intelligent, competent, and knows it.

I told him to consider the possibility that the accident was no accident. I created a sequence that came from Primary Triangle 7 about letting go of pride and aligning with the spiritual gift of humility. I encouraged him to recontextualize the events of the past year as an opportunity to grow spiritually and, from that positionality, the fall was a gift, a kind of wake-up call.

I reviewed all of the sequences that were imprinted, asking the Inner Teacher if he needed to continue to imprint them. IBFRT indicated that he should recite four of the sequences at least ten times, two or three times a day, until his next appointment on Wednesday. I also told him that he needed to do his spiritual work. He went back to the hotel with my second book. He read the meditations and did his numbers.

On Monday, he *walked* into the clinic. He was so excited that he just wanted us to know what had happened. No scooter! He told Ardith that in the hotel there was not much to do except recite the numerical sequences and read the meditations. He did the sequences for *hours* at a time. We were very happy and excited for him. Ardith told him that I would test him again on Wednesday.

On Wednesday, some additional sequences were created to rebuild the bone. There was little pain and no scooter. The wound which had been open for over a year was beginning to close. He told me that he didn't realize I was so "spiritual." He enjoyed how he felt doing the meditations and sequences. When I calibrated him this time, he was over 500 on the Hawkins MOC, and his primary coherence triangle was no longer in Primary Triangle 3 but was now located in Primary Triangle 5. This is a contextual field in which healing may take place, on the outside *and the inside*.

He continued to do the sequences and meditations. On Saturday, the day he returned to Florida, I retested him. He was solidly located within Primary Triangle 5. I imprinted and gave him two more sequences. When he returned to be examined by the doctors in Florida, they told him that the infection in his foot was gone. He told us that it was impossible to explain to the doctors what had taken place.

Several weeks later, he was informed that his mitral valve was damaged so severely by intravenous antibiotics that he needed the valve to be replaced. He decided to fly back to see me with the hope that there was an alternative to surgery. I saw him once. The triangles were used to lead to a location from which to create a sequence to regenerate the mitral valve. A second sequence was created to remove the stress of bacteria that were affecting the heart. I was pleased to also find that his overall level of consciousness was even more solidly grounded in Primary Triangle Five. With the same diligence, he did his sequences and meditations. Three weeks later, the medical experts told him that it was a miracle. They had not seen anything like it. The mitral valve was completely restored and the surgery was cancelled. He told the doctors that he came up to see that "guy in Wisconsin" for help.

Additional Comments About Example Three

Healing comes through recontextualization. While the imprinting was powerful, the healing required the patient to let go of the limiting beliefs of an accident victim. I believe there was a great inner awakening that occurred through difficult events, including the possibility of losing his foot. While the accident was contextualized as a physical event requiring a physical intervention, there was a deeper meaning and opportunity for healing of body and spirit.

Beyond Two Positionalities

While the starting points may differ, there is no essential difference between the two uses of the tool because the separation between the physical and non-physical is an illusion. The starting point for the testing is quite arbitrary, and reflects only the limitations of perception.

While many problems appear to be only, or mostly, physical, and other struggles appear to be only, or mostly, non-physical, the differentiation is of little significance. The formalism of sharing these two approaches with the reader is an attempt to systematize the application of whisperology to render it more understandable. What appears to be demonstrated through the three examples is that health is most appreciated as coherence within and between all seven bodies.

How does the recognition of two equally valid starting points give rise to a new positionality about the use of The Figure? Instead of deciding which starting point is better, based on what appears to be a physical or a non-physical issue, one may use IBFRT to determine where to begin testing and imprinting. How is this done? As simple and straightforward as it sounds! No matter what the reason may be, the tester uses IBFRT to determine what form of incoherence is the most helpful starting point. The intention that surrenders the primacy of any approach based on what the tester knows is humbly set aside, in order to simply be as open as possible to where the Great Unseen leads the tester. At the beginning of every test, when I place my hands on someone else's ankles, silently I pray "Let us honor what God is manifesting in and through this person." I ask if there is permission to test the person. With every step, I ask if there is permission to continue testing to determine if the point is reached for the person when no additional imprinting is required to help her. I may also receive a message that the capacity for what the person can handle during the session has been reached.

This is the best approach in every testing situation because the only rule is to listen for and humbly accept the guidance of a divine whisper. When testing and imprinting is guided by this intention there can be no confusion about who is doing the healing. At best, one realizes that God can use any of us as a vehicle of grace.

When asking what space to focus upon without presuming to know the most helpful course of action, and what needs to be accomplished, a path of least resistance appears. With faith, humility, and love as the only guides to select the primary triangle, the best path for healing shines forth. We do not choose the path but rather the creator of the path has a magical way of helping us to find it! One might call it a butterfly path, meaning a welcomed and peaceful intervention where the whole system is not changed by force but through the power of a whisper, a gentle flutter of wings. In this instance, it appears that the butterfly is not circumscribed by The Figure but lies beyond its perimeter in Universal Consciousness, a field that encompasses the seven primary triangles. As if by magic, a humble intention invites the butterfly to enter human consciousness and transform what seems immutable in time space.

CONCLUSION
Evolution of Whisperology

What is described in this book is a technology of consciousness that I call whisperology. This *consciousness-based technology* is superluminal and operates beyond the confines of space time. And it now includes a new tool for the wondrous world of whisperology—a beautiful constellation of triangles called The Figure!

There is so much that we believe we know and build a world upon, yet even with the best of Human's sophisticated tools, only the surface has been scratched. Impressive human achievements are easily recontextualized and "brought down to size" by a simple experiment that Bill Tiller describes in his book, *Some Science Adventures with Real Magic*:

"In a dual camera, rigid tripod mounting with a single shutter release switch experiment, wherein one camera was a normal, unsensitized camera while the other was sensitized by lengthy exposure to the biofield of a very special person, pictures were taken that appeared normal for the unsensitized camera but strikingly anomalous for the biofield-sensitized camera. In particular, often (1) normally opaque human bodies, revealed by the unsensitized camera, were semi-transparent to reveal objects on the wall behind such bodies, by the sensitized camera or (2) normal pictures of light wells and chairs in a room, revealed by the unsensitized camera, contained waving streamers or ribbons of light from the light wells and rising plumes of light from the chairs in the photos from the sensitized camera. Further, in a single sensitized camera on the tripod experiment, with the plastic lens still covering the lens, relatively bright and detailed pictures of the room appeared in the photos.

In all of this, the intention held by this very special person was just 'to reveal God's universe.'"[149]

This experiment encourages me to offer still one more analogy about The Figure. The Figure is like a lens—a "heptafocal" lens—that sees seven bodies, in the form of seven primary triangles when the lens wearer looks at Human. The lens recognizes the objects within all of the bodies which are invisible to the conventional lens of science and materialism. The context of the wearer of this magical lens sees a different reality which is not obscured by a lens cover or a limiting belief system. Of course, the heptafocal vision cannot be awakened and used without an expansion of context. I would invite the reader to consider The Figure as a tool of "real magic."

In whisperology, *the fundamental partition of space* is into 63 self-similar triangles, a spatial network, referred to as simply The Figure. Many terms have been tested to attempt to describe the nature of the seven primary triangles, and the nine triangles which comprise each primary triangle. According to IBFRT, the most useful and conscious de-

---

[149] Tiller, William A., Dibble, Walter E., and Fandel, Gregory. *Some Science Adventures With Real Magic* (Pavior Publishing, Walnut Creek, California: 2005) p. 11.

scriptions of the triangles include the following concepts: manifestations of the unmanifest, seven bodies, seven densities, seven levels, seven spatial networks, a contextual map, a human coherence map, and the image and likeness of the Creator. The simple analogies of likening The Figure to an antenna, a prism, or a lens are intended to encourage the reader to a deeper understanding and appreciation that beyond the world of appearances, and at the highest level of consciousness, all of creation shares an intrinsic connection and fundamental oneness.

Using IBFRT, the tools of whisperology, including The Figure, appear to be highly compatible with the author's understanding of Tillerian physics, the Hawkins' MOC, Christian mysticism, and many of the theories of Eastern spirituality. There is very little, if any, significant compatibility with conventional medicine.

I want to conclude the book by reviewing the primary aspects of the structure of The Figure and its application in whisperology. Anything that is included in the book to describe the geometry of the whisper comes from the guidance and endorsement of the Inner Teacher.

Healing is manifested from the non-linear realm that resolves perceptions about content through connection with a higher domain of consciousness. The non-linear domains are holy and spiritual places filled with an unlimited amount of grace. Healing restores coherence in all domains including subtle bodies, not just the physical body.

Pain and ill health are the manifestation of a lack of coherency. It would appear that in many instances, if we move outside of the space time network, we may be able to see that our "troubles" occur as a manifestation of an incoherent, non-integrous intention. Therefore, the healing of the incoherency occurs through alignment with an integrous intention that becomes available as a gift from a higher context. The expanded context alters perception and the content of what appeared to have been "the problem" is changed. The triangles assist in the location of the proper space to establish a coherent connection with a higher context, a more inclusive and powerful geometry, in which healing can take place.

Incoherent conditions that eventually manifest as stress, emotional or physical symptoms, and disease are removed through a contextual shift. Incoherence is not a content problem to be solved; *it is a contextual limitation to be overcome through the expansion of the context which gives the perceived problem a different meaning instead of* reworking the same content, over and over again. The expansion of context occurs through the surrender of misperceptions, or limiting beliefs that serve to keep the person stuck, unable to move beyond the current state of affairs. *Healing is the outcome of recontextualization.*

Health is complete coherency with the Creator on every level: spiritual, mental, and emotional, not just physical. From the inside to the outside, from the spiritual to the earthly, every aspect of our being is completely aligned, completely coherent with the Creator and the Divine Intention that resulted in the incarnation of a soul into the body. From the perspective of whisperology, informational structures and energetic structures—not the physical organs, tissues, and cells—become the central focus of human evolution. The physical "stuff" is the least of our problems because health comes from within. From the standpoint of emergence, then, as many others have said, we will manifest physically what we hold in mind. The mind is the most powerful tool the Creator has given us.

Incoherence in any aspect of human existence, establishes a limiting context for health that goes beyond the boundaries of considering the physical body to be the key to learning how to care for ourselves, or considering the physical body as the producer instead of the transmitter of other aspects of our being. We will be what we choose to be, each day we get up and decide how we will spend our day. *Our thoughts are the ultimate epigenetic tool.* There can be no higher science than one that seeks to be aligned with the spiritual laws of the universe. The word *coherency* expresses this intention and goal.

Whisperology continues to be a useful description for the theories and applications of IBFRT. The power, magnification, and geometry of the whisper are the most helpful phrases that express the new adventures in the land of whisperology. The journey to this context required me to surrender an attachment to the content of what I think, or thought I knew, so that the Creator might show me how little I know, and thrill me with the possibility of being a more faithful servant. My intellect participates in the process but only as a servant, not as the boss. These days I don't spend much time wondering what others think about the value of what I am being given, who is providing the assistance, or the lack of "objective" scientific standards. Spiritual truths that are not perceptible are likely never to be accepted by conventional science.

"The land beyond 499," as David Hawkins refers to it, operates according to laws that are inaccessible to current technologies and the consciousness that has built them. In the form of a whisper, through the power of intention, the new information is imprinted through the hands to the patient. The Hawkins' MOC has not been reproduced in The Figure but has served as an invaluable resource and additional frame of reference for IBFRT. I am deeply indebted to Hawkins and realize that many of the building blocks of whisperology would not be possible without his assistance. Whisperology makes no claim to be a complete or accurate depiction of the genius of Hawkins' theories.

The transfer of information is believed to occur within the non-linear domain and simultaneously manifests its power in the linear world of space time. For Tiller, the coupling between D-space and R-space substances, to condition space and create a higher level of coherence between the various bodies of Human, translates his theoretical framework into action through specific tuning of his intention host devices (IHDs) to accomplish integrous goals. The expansion of consciousness that takes place in the patient manifests within all of the "bodies" of the patient, including the one that is called the physical body. Bill and Jean Tiller's friendship and encouragement to keep working with The Figure, but with my own methods and Inner Teacher, has been invaluable. From my perspective, I see where our ideas appear to be perfectly in sync with each other, but also the places where perhaps we may see things differently. I do not intend in any way to presume, or have the reader assume, that I speak for Bill or The Tiller Institute. I do wish to acknowledge as clearly as possible that my work has been influenced not only by his work but our friendship, second to none.

Beyond the perceptual world and all the theories developed to describe its origin and content, there are other worlds, not to be described as physical worlds. Consciousness dwells in the spiritual world, not the orderly or chaotic aspects of the physical world. We originate from the spiritual world and when we are finished with the use of the bio-body suit, we return Home. The spiritual world is not a fractal playground. The essential structure is symmetrical and not defined by fashionable irregularity. There is perfect self-similarity in the spiritual world because everything is made in the image and likeness of the Creator. Nothing in mathematics or physics can apprehend what the familiar phrase from Genesis expresses about the connectedness between the divine and the human and its presence in the entire universe.

Leave it to the mystic, or the person of simple faith, the spiritually evolved soul, to simply affirm what is *subjectively* obvious. It simply is. This is the greatest context that a human may experience and live by that does not change whether life is viewed up close or far away. Everything is organized and patterned by the hand of the Creator, including you and me.

What does this pattern, this image and likeness of the Creator, look like? How does it "appear" in the physical world? The essential pattern does not appear in the physical world but rather is found above it, below it, in front of it, behind it, permeating it. We can appreciate the beauty and symmetry of the appearance of creation in the symbol and figure of an isosceles triangle, the capital letter *delta*, the fourth letter in the Greek alphabet, meaning "change." The symbol of change is the expression of incarnation. From space with no structure, a structure emerges that calls attention to a particular region of partitioned space by inscribing the seamless fabric of nothingness with three lines to create a home for something. There is the beginning of something, a single Word becoming flesh. There is a cascade of orderly, self-similar partitions that establish the heavens and the earth. If we imagine ourselves to be outside an infinitely large triangular space, there is only the unknowable deep of the Creator.

In two dimensions, the abstraction used to express the structuring of space is a triangle. The creation of the triangle changes space. Now there is an inside and an outside, light and darkness, day and night, above and below, East and West, heaven and earth, potential and actual, an endless proliferation of self-similar spaces that reflect the Creator. Each space, from the smallest to the largest, is a contextual neighborhood that establishes the boundaries of content that belongs within its boundaries, or somewhere else.

Since every aspect and scale of the physical world is permeated by the triangular network, The Figure invites its user to employ the new tool as a universal map, to find out where you are, and help you to find your destination; or alternatively, like a series of completely catalogued libraries, where everything, in any scale, is organized and discovered within the perfect space.

Correspondences are plentiful, safely inexhaustible, when the connections between the spiritual world and the material world are realized through the use of the map. The Figure steers us away from the limited perception of a captivated but limited view of only a physical world so that we might contemplate the essence of the physical world, where the objective gives way to the subjective.

The Figure appears to be a useful tool to appreciate the manifestation of the Unmanifest, on any scale, including planet Earth. We have more in common with a plant or a honeybee than we realize! The image and likeness of the Creator is in every aspect of the universe. Every creature, every human, every entity, bears this mark. In every manifestation, small and large, the image and likeness of the Creator is present. In the manifested universe, every bit of it has a temporal and eternal aspect. What all manifestations share in common is not a material substance, a God particle (unless the magical particle is appreciated as a metaphor), but rather a unifying purpose. While every individual purpose is unique, all creation carries within it a unifying divine purpose. Divine purpose is what all creation shares in common because it's part of the grand design. *To be created in the image and likeness of the Creator means to be created for a purpose. The essential purpose is to manifest its essence.* The *particular* purpose and function will be unique for every entity, or portion of an entity. What links them all together is the unifying essence of the Creator in all of creation, large or small, simple or complex.

And what of Human? Humans, unlike rocks, plants, or giraffes, do not remain intrinsically aligned with the divine purpose. Every human has the ability to deviate from her purpose, to separate herself from the purpose for which she came into being, *through the exercise of freedom, to refuse to be, or remain, aligned.* It is the most common and apparently necessary path. Yet even this refusal will serve a larger purpose. The primary intention in this book is to explore and apply this tool for the human entity which resides *in*, not *on* Mother Earth, known as *homo sapiens*, and for all of us to experience home. Yes, *Home.* This is the ultimate purpose of the tool in the first place.

The Figure is of great value because it reveals hidden information that may be used by Human to eliminate incoherent conditions and misperceptions that are experienced as problems on many levels of awareness. The Figure helps its users to find the way Home. "So by faith, hope, and love, by the power of intention and the gift of grace, let us walk in the Light, reflect the Light, become One with the Light. Let us be restored and transformed by the Light. For the Light is our source, our destination, and our home."[150]

The governing structure includes a temporal purpose that is housed in the temporal aspect which manifests the eternal essence and design. The way forward to a deeper understanding and wisdom of these two aspects, the temporal and the eternal, leads to further reflection about the primacy of our love, and the opportunity to use the intellect to understand the spiritual laws of the universe. The wedded functions of creation and evolution express divine Intention. We find these complementary functions in the Ten Commandments, as well as other spiritual traditions. Understanding and wisdom cannot be separated from the governing love in a human life. This is the meaning of the first, and most important (governing), commandment: *Thou shalt have no other gods before me.*

If we look around us, we can see how small and foolish, or how large and wise, the governing love is, within a particular person, or community, or nation. The commandments tell us what we must love, and what we must not love, so that our intelligence and volition serve to align the temporal with the eternal, our experience of life on earth. The first commandment is the guiding purpose that ensures "thy will be done on earth as it is in heaven." In this way, the commandments are a guideline to create life at its highest level by connecting the creation and evolution of every life together, from beginning to end, from inner to outer, from potential to creative evolution. This is the movement from the seventh group of triangles to the first group of triangles in its temporal and eternal aspects. The lost is found and returns Home with an awakened and transformed awareness of freedom and purpose.

What is being described through all of my books, dear reader, is *a functional path, a path of spiritual development.* In one sense, the path to the Creator moves in two directions. Humans evolve, moving out into

---

[150] Tonsager, *Intention Based Field Resonance Testing: The Magnification of the Whisper*, p. 126

the world through the realization of their individual purposes. If these purposes are aligned with the spiritual laws of the universe, *then human expansion also moves inwardly* because there is an inner knowing... that there is full alignment with the image and likeness of the Creator. The divine purpose in each person is fulfilled through this path.

The relationship between the temporal aspect and the eternal aspect is appreciated through function. A hierarchy of function is applicable to the temporal world at any microscopic or macroscopic level including the human body. The spiritual laws govern the temporal and eternal spaces. Health, physical and spiritual, comes from the Creator.

Thus, we can do no better than to consciously choose to humbly align ourselves with divine intention. *Health is created through the daily choices that reflect the quality of our thinking that is based on the integrous intention that "Thy will be done on earth as it is in heaven."*

I know little, if anything significant, about the land beyond The Figure because it is the domain of the angels and distant realities of universal consciousness. Hawkins assigned numbers well beyond 1,000 to calibrate the consciousness of these realities, although I wonder if these numbers are simply an acknowledgement of something well beyond human comprehension and experience. Nonetheless, what we know or believe to be worthy of the designation Human is connected with an infinitely more powerful reality, whether the species knows it or not. The Figure captures nearly, but not all of what is essential to the health of Human, perhaps as much as 95 percent. The most critical part may well be in the unexplored 5 percent. For the time being, a few messages of connection are being exchanged with the hope of a deepened awareness of a universal connection to Human and beyond. The whisper does not fade into nothing, but travels farther and deeper into its Home.

MEDITATION

This is the day that the Lord has made.
Let us rejoice and be glad in it.
Let us give thanks for the gift of The Light.
For it is The Light that makes us One.
All has come from The Light.
And, one day all will return.
So, let us give thanks for gifts of faith, hope, and love.
For when The Light has come into our lives
The world is forgiven.
There are no grievances.
About anyone or anything
For any reason.
Known or unknown,
Future, present, past, or karmic
It matters not.
For, in the brilliance of The Light,
Our spiritual vision is restored.
And we honor the One Light.
That stands behind and beyond

Permeating every appearance including our own.
And we give thanks for the gift of peace.
Peace which comes when we surrender
Every resistance to The Light.
So, by faith, hope, and love
By the power of intention
And the gift of grace,
Let us walk in The Light,
Reflect The Light,
Become one with The Light.
For The Light is our destination
And our Home.
I am more than a body.
I am free.
An infinite Being subject only to what I hold in mind.
And still as God intended me to be.
And to become.
Fully found.
Fully free.
Fully awakened.
Fully transformed.

FIGURES

Figure 1.
"The Figure"

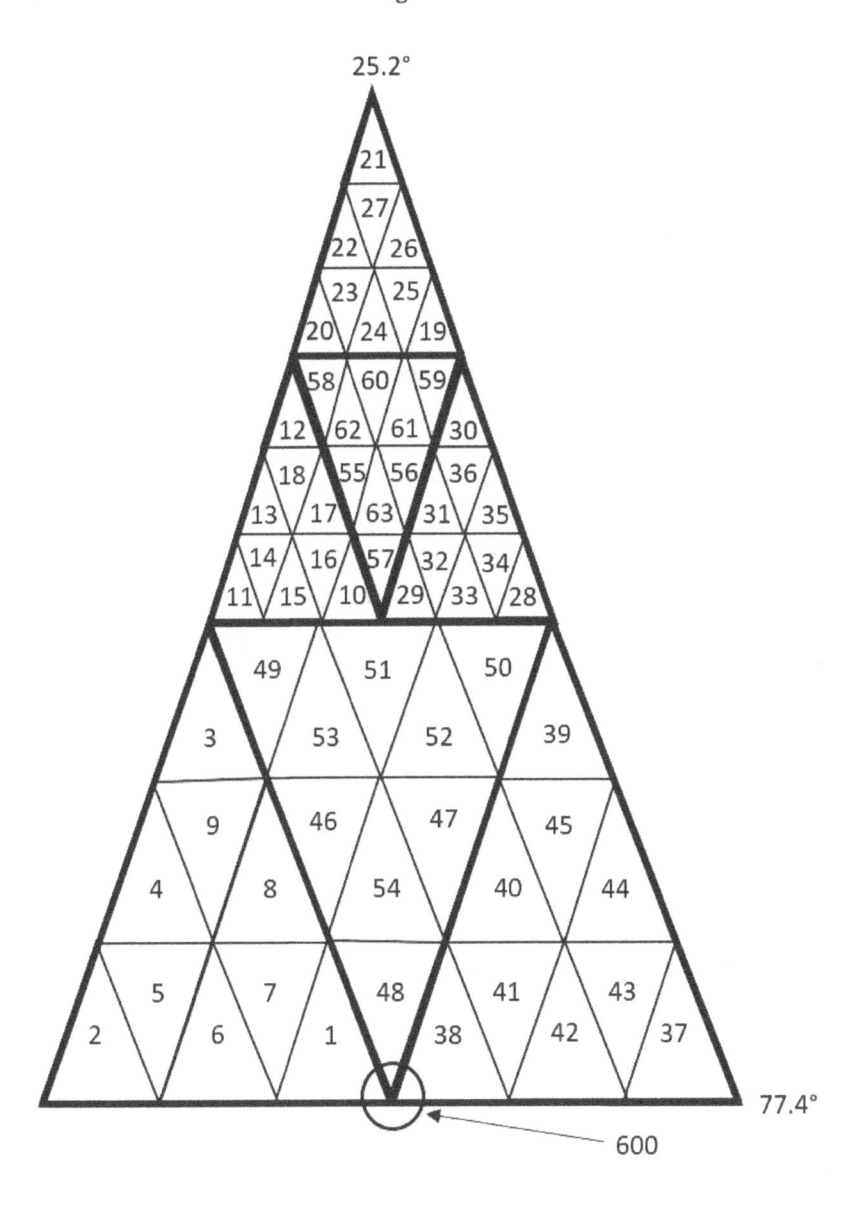

Intention Based Field Resonance Testing • 175

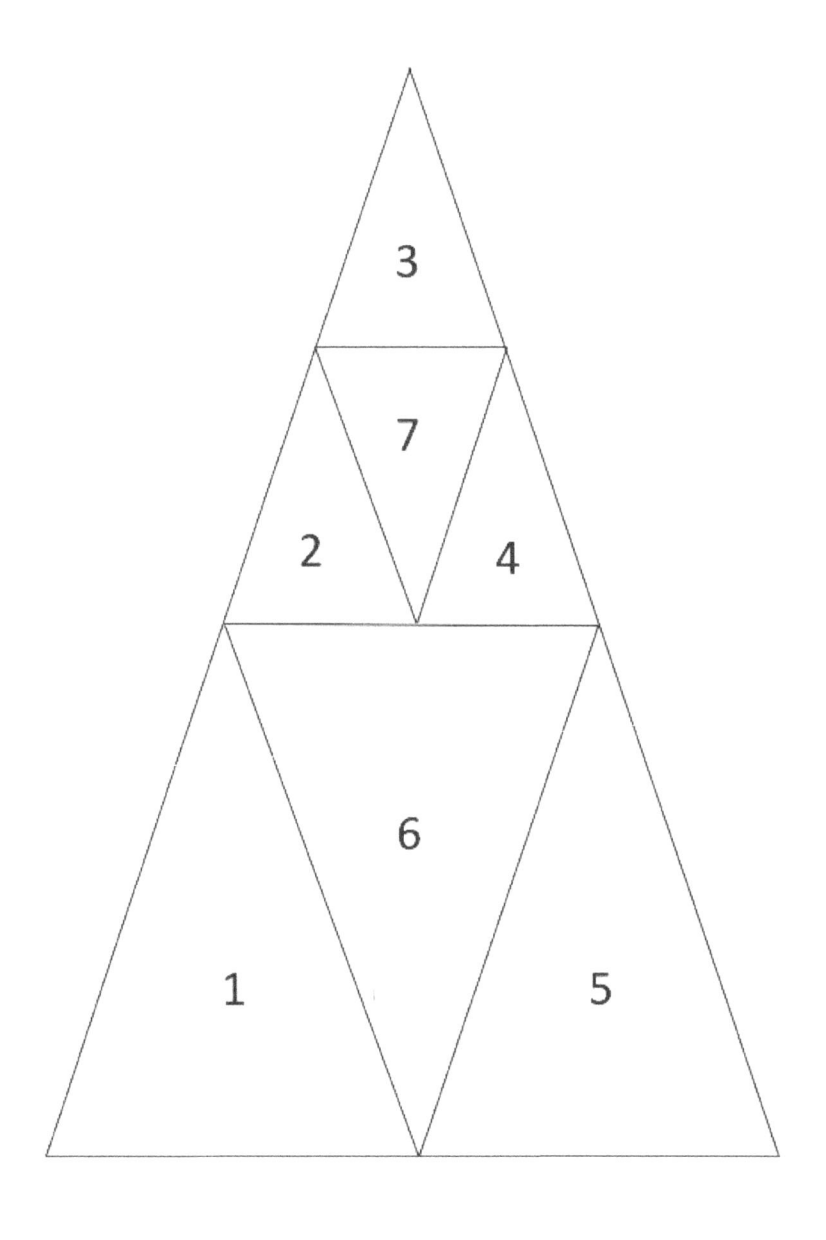

Figure 2.
"The Seven Primary Triangles"

Steven R Tonsager • 176

Figure 3.
"The 9 Triangles in a Primary Triangle"

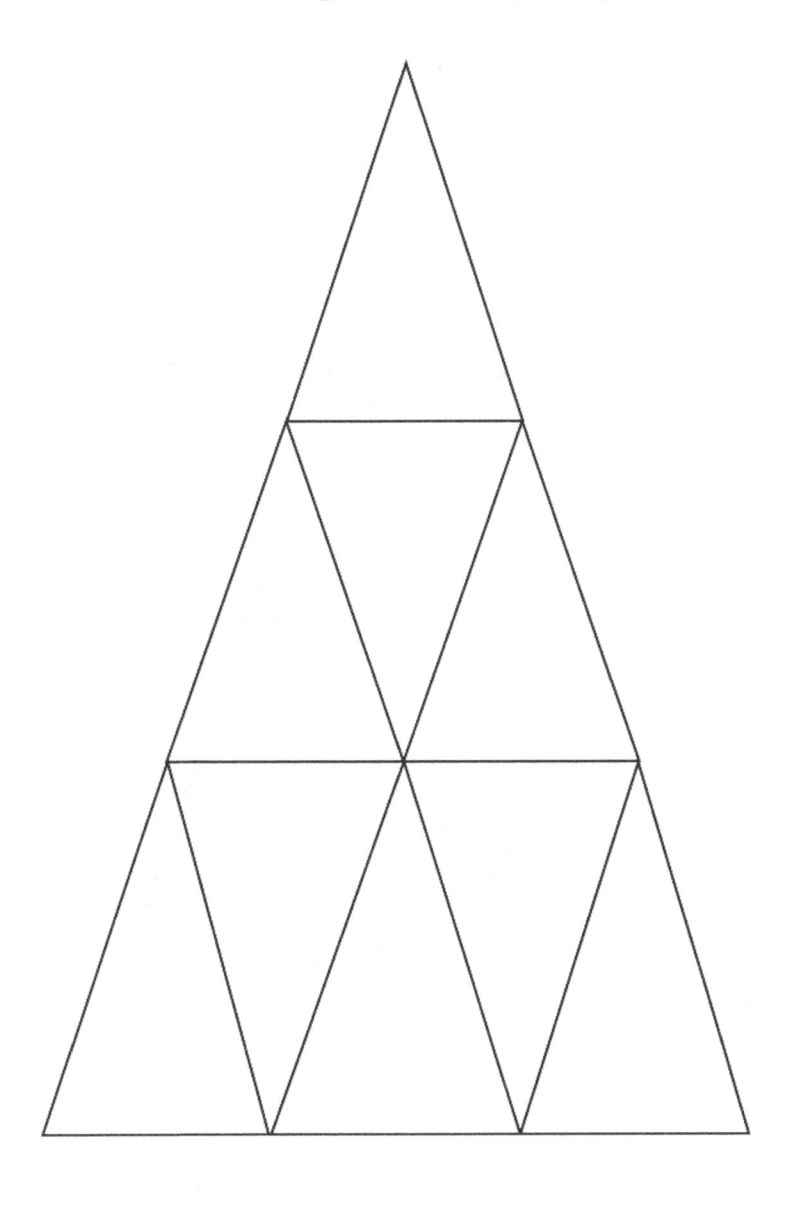

Figure 4.
"The Correlation Between the Figure and Seven Chakras"

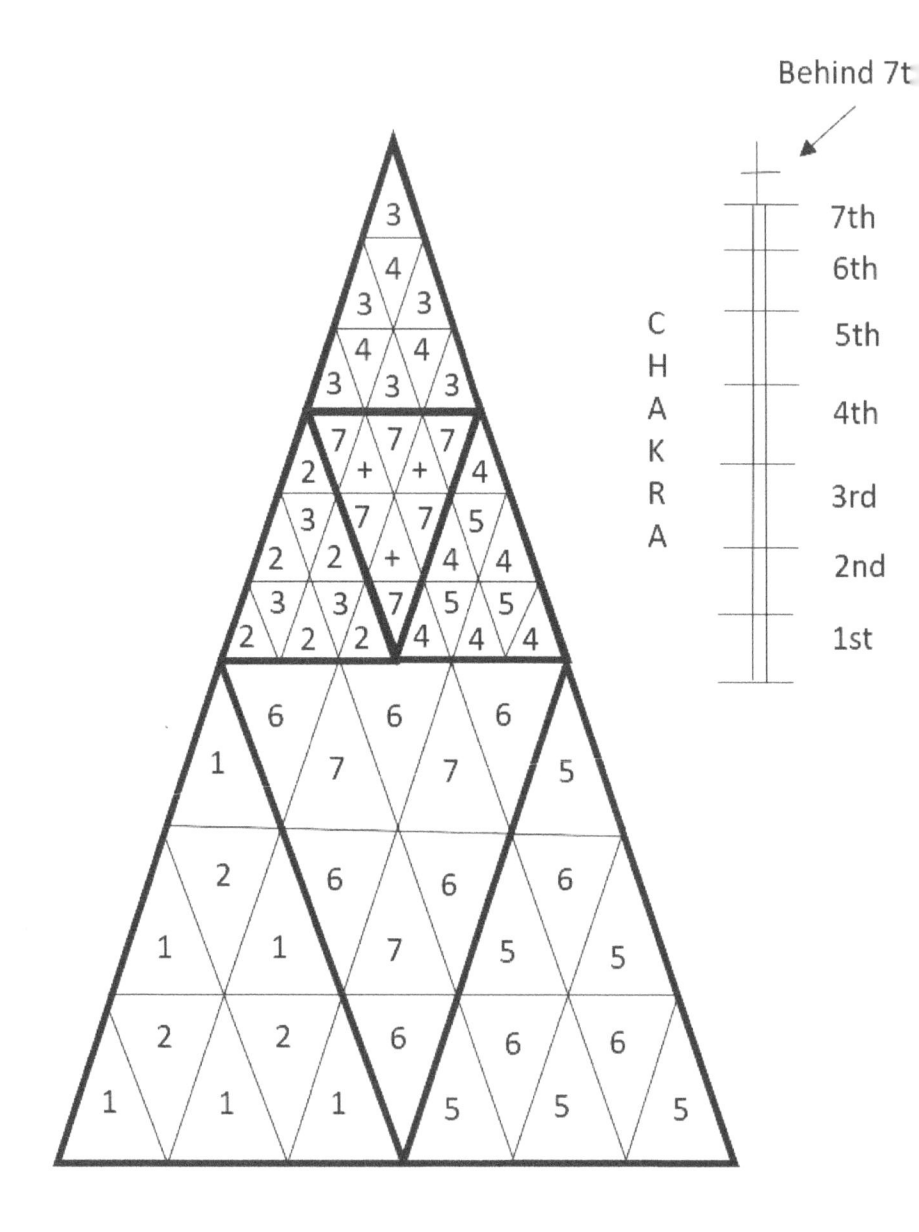

Steven R Tonsager • 178

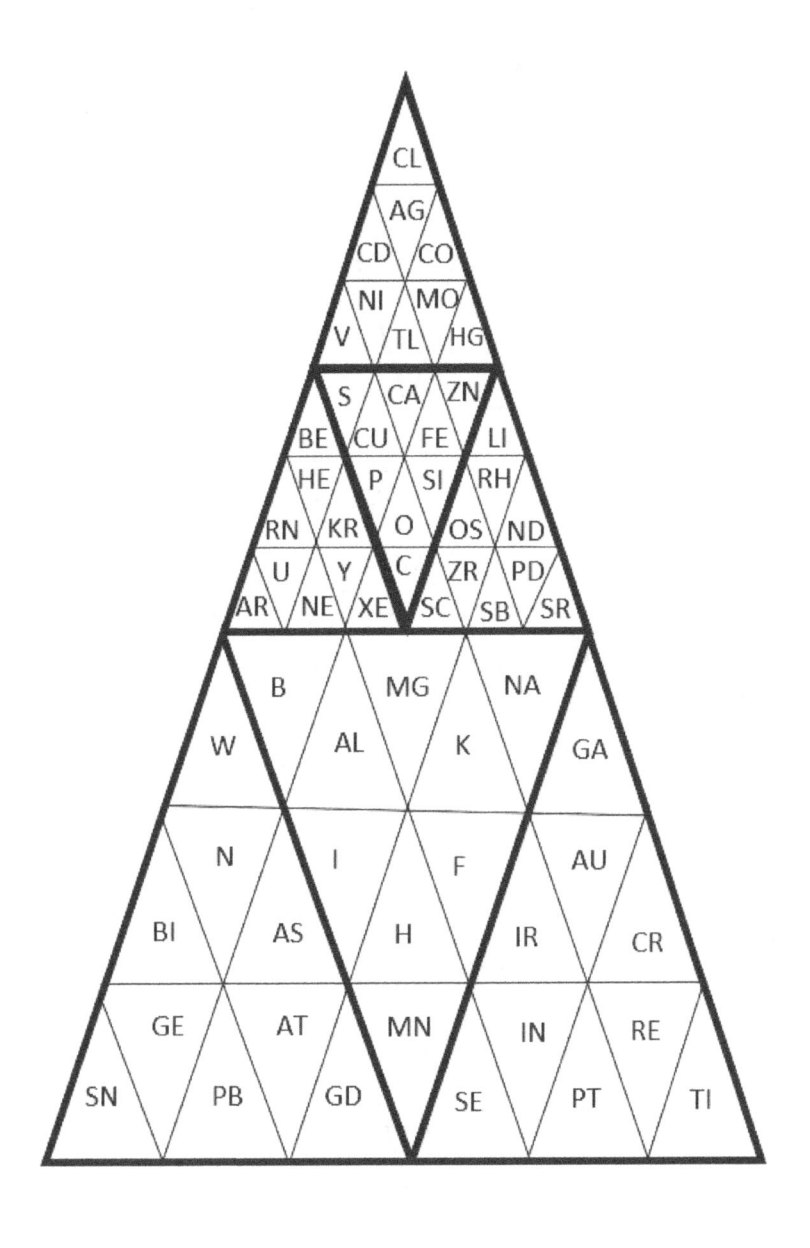

Figure 5.
"Correlation of Elements with the Figure"

Intention Based Field Resonance Testing • 179

Figure 6.
"Correlation of Spiritual Gifts with the Figure"

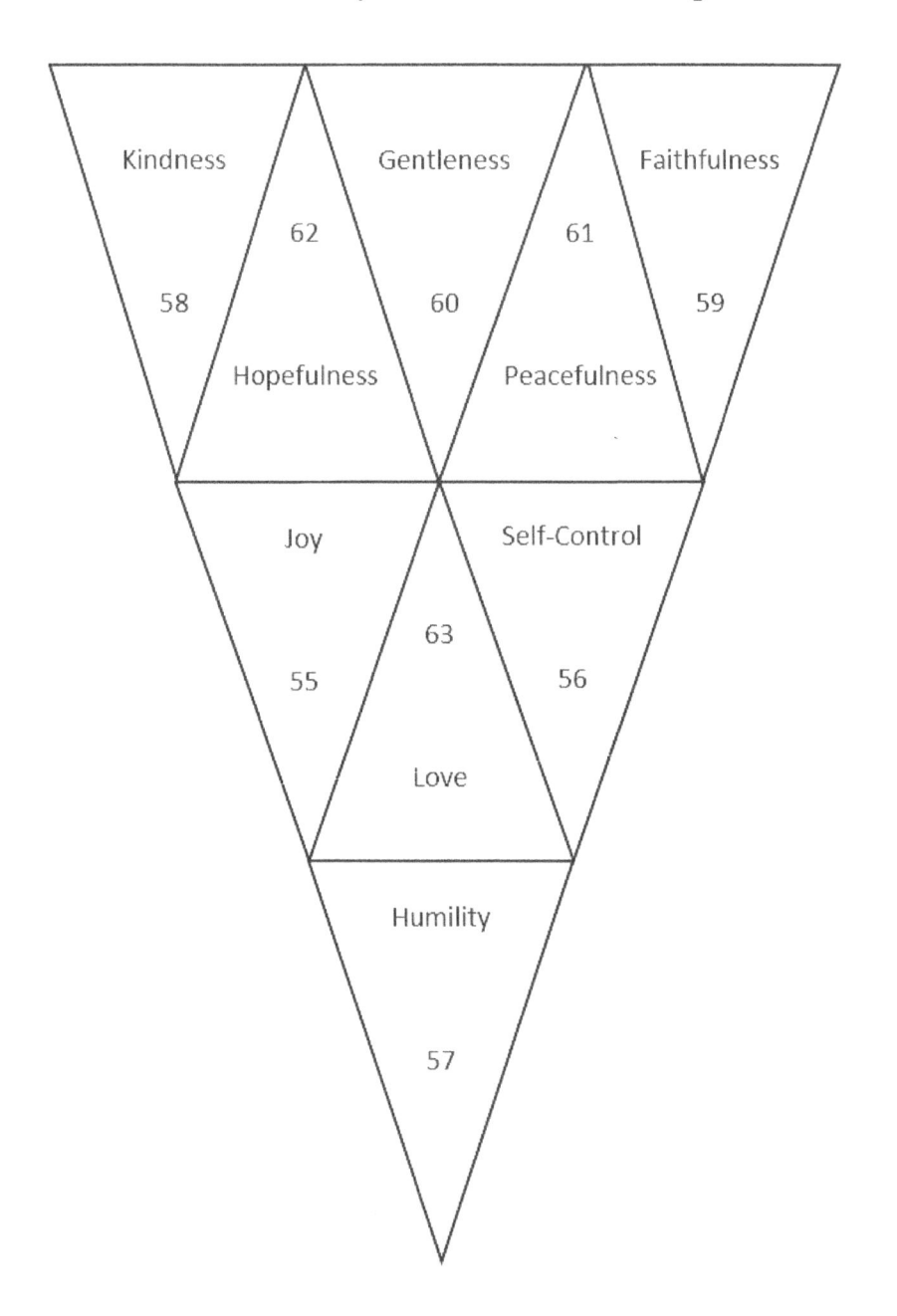

Kindness
Gentleness
Faithfulness
62
61
58
60
59
Hopefulness
Peacefulness
Joy
Self-Control
63
55
56
Love
Humility
57

Steven R Tonsager • 180

Figure 7.
"Maggie's Test"
The Seven Primary Triangles"

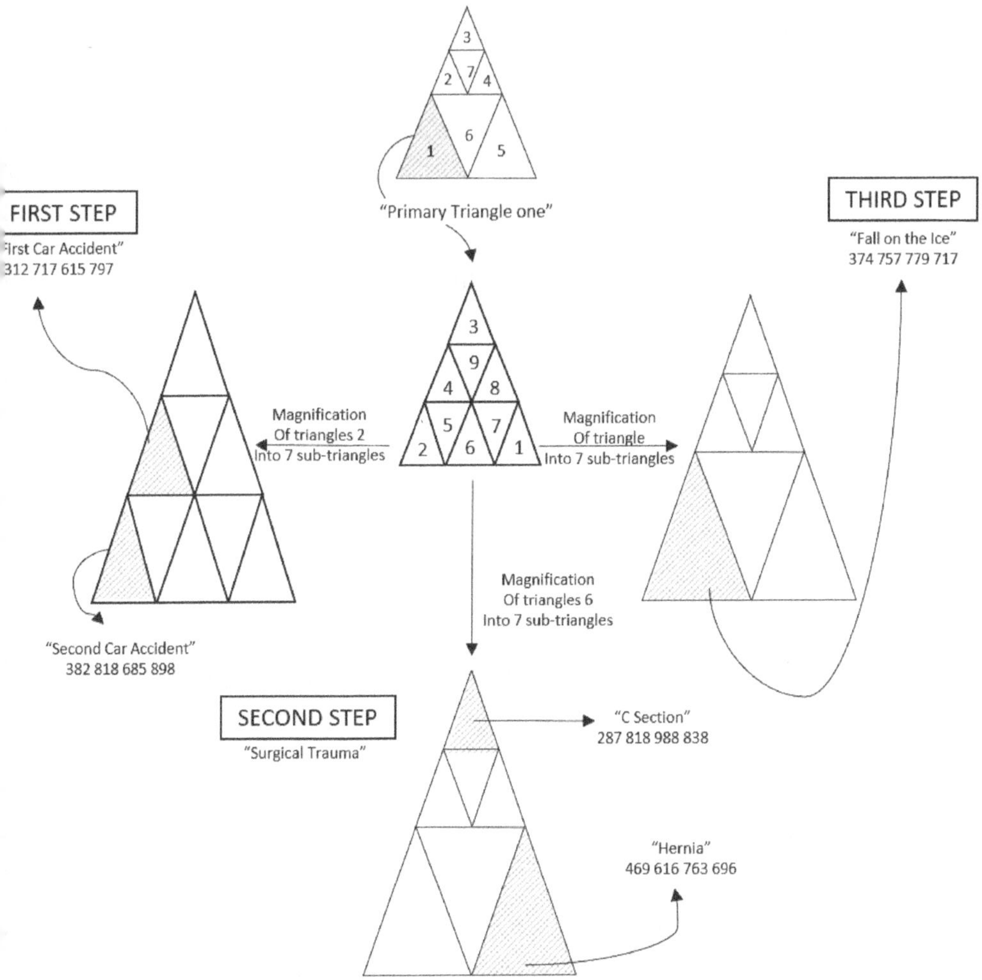

"Primary Triangle one"

FIRST STEP
"First Car Accident"
312 717 615 797

"Second Car Accident"
382 818 685 898

Magnification
Of triangles 2
Into 7 sub-triangles

Magnification
Of triangle
Into 7 sub-triangles

THIRD STEP
"Fall on the Ice"
374 757 779 717

Magnification
Of triangles 6
Into 7 sub-triangles

SECOND STEP
"Surgical Trauma"

"C Section"
287 818 988 838

"Hernia"
469 616 763 696

Intention Based Field Resonance Testing ♦ 181

Figure 8.
"Ted's Test"

Triangle 6

Division into 7 sub-triangles

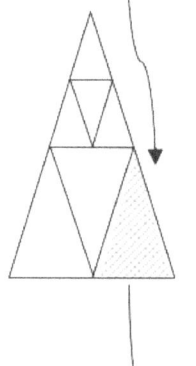

Division of Shaded Sub-Triangles
Into 9 "Sub Sub" Triangles

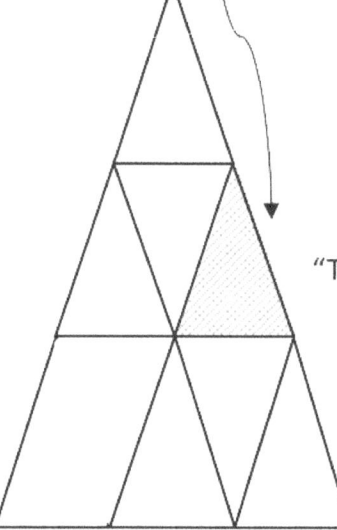

Location of
"Ted's Titanium Related Knee Replacement"

GLOSSARY

Algorithm. A method, set of rules, or instruction used in IBFRT to test and treat the client.

Applied Kinesiology. A field of study and application that allows the elucidation of information through various forms of muscle test. In contrast to many forms of Applied Kinesiology (AK), IBFRT testing does not rely upon a physical challenge of a strong intact muscle to elucidate helpful information. IBFRT gathers information through a dowsing response that is experienced by the tester by a subjective physical indicator. A conventional use of AK may be used to help the client to appreciate the influence of incoherence and its resolution at times to enhance the understanding of the client. This is useful but not part of whisperology. Sometimes referred to as "the dog and pony show," the intention is only to promote greater understanding for the client when this appears to be useful.

Broadcast. IBFRT uses the term to describe the sending of an intention to a remote target, that is, a person who is not *physically* present for direct testing or treatment. Intention may be broadcast in a variety of ways to known and unknown individuals or groups. See Dr. Tiller's books for powerful examples of broadcasting intention.

Cleared or clearing. A stress identified by the testing response has been eliminated.

Coherence. The presence of a harmonious state of a particular quality (physical, emotional, spiritual, etc.), within a particular context (solar, organ system, organ, cell, elemental, etc.). The coherence is subjectively experienced by the practitioner as truthful and without stress.

Collective Karma. The aspect of karma which is connected to the community, tribe, race, or culture in which the individual has been educated and imprinted, consciously and unconsciously. The term is intended to include more than immediate family including parents, grandparents, and recent ancestors. This would include previous lifetimes and the vast influences from ancient history.

Content. The specific thoughts, feelings, beliefs, and positionalities which are reflective of a contextual frame of reference. While people may use exactly the same words to describe their perceptions, the meaning is often different because people often do not operate from the same context. IBFRT symbolizes the content as the space within a triangle.

Context. The frame of reference conscious and unconsciously held by a person, a community, or a culture which determines what may be perceived and regarded as true. IBFRT symbolizes context as the three lines which define the space and create the boundaries for content.

Deltope. IBFRT uses this newly created word to describe the measurement of intensity of intention. Deltopes are increased when the ego "gets out of the way." The power of intention, the gift of grace, and God's infinite love are received with openness and humility. Deltopes are increased by a group of "like-minded intenders" and clarity of the intention, which may be enhanced through a shared intention statement or numerical sequence.

Deltron. Dr. William A. Tiller postulated a type of particle or substance which he called a deltron to be that which connected R-space (reciprocal space-time) with D-space (space-time). Deltron theory provided an ingenious means to explain, without violating Einstein's relativity theory or the laws of thermodynamics, how intention could affect the physical world.

Deltron Bridge. IBFRT uses the term to refer to the power of integrous intention and an evolved consciousness to affect the physical world through the power of intention. With regard to this book, the primary emphasis is that deltrons are the genius of Dr. William A. Tiller's theories to help others to recognize a means in which positive emotions, especially love, create coherence in the physical world—which is believed by most scientists to not be influenced from another realm that is not measurable through scientific methodologies.

Downward Causation. A theory which believes that the creation of all things begins from "above," in a non-material or non-linear realm, with the final manifestation occurring in the material or linear realm. The non-linear realm does not operate according to conventional science and the space time realm. The linear realm is physical and operates according to the laws of conventional physics within space time.

Drills. The practices of an IBFRT practitioner to increase consciousness for spiritual growth.

Electromagnetic Field (EMF) Stress. EMF stress includes the man-made radiation produced by devices like cell phones, computers, and fluorescent lights. However, there are many other sources of this form of stress, including disturbances to the Schumann Resonance. IBFRT recognizes EMF stress as a source of incoherence.

Elemental Coherence. A type of coherence that exists between a person and an element. The element is believed to not only include its chemical and physical properties, but its spiritual qualities. Elemental coherence as it is developed through IBFRT finds elemental coherence to express fundamental connections between an element and the person within the body, as well as to forces outside of the body, including the earth, moon, and sun.

Figure (The Figure). The 2-dimensional representation which shows a fundamental pattern of 63 isosceles triangles. The Figure is an impersonal spiritual structure within consciousness that is created by consciousness so that a local entity may understand itself, explore its level of consciousness, its relationship to consciousness, and experience the Life Force.

H Vial. IBFRT uses this description to designate a bottle containing water that has been imprinted solely by the power of intention to carry the qualities of that intention. This is done through the imprinting of the target solely through the power of intention. There are no limitations regarding the target but is commonly used to develop a vial for testing and/or treatment. The designation *bottle* and *vial* are used interchangeably. The H is a reference to honor the work of David Hawkins.

Iatrogenic Factors/Iatrogenic Conditions. The terms refer to unintended or unanticipated outcomes through a medical intervention, which was only intended to bring a useful benefit but has introduced some form of incoherence. Common examples of these unwelcomed outcomes include responses to a medication, treatment, or test.

IBFRT. Intention Based Field Resonance Testing.

Incoherence. The presence of a disharmonious state of a particular quality (physical, emotional, spiritual, etc.) within a particular context (solar, organ system, organ, cell, elemental, etc.). The incoherence is subjectively experienced by the practitioner as not truthful and stressful.

Intact Muscle. In Applied Kinesiology, this refers to a muscle that remains strong against a physical challenge.

Individual Karma. That aspect of oneself which is part of the spiritual inheritance for an individual life. Alignment with the purpose of a particular incarnation, or the failure to do so, manifests divine justice which is perfect and complete. Depending on the choices that are made, there is the accumulation of positive or negative karma.

Isode. A homeopathic remedy that is made from a pernicious agent (toxin, virus, heavy metal, cell phone emission, allergen, etc.) or an environmental source that may contain harmful pathogenic factors. Examples of environmental sources include urine, stool, saliva, well water, exhaust emission, the air in a barn, and an extracted tooth.

Kidney 27. An acupuncture point located on the chest. The specific location is on the lower border of the clavicle, 2 *cun* lateral to the anterior midline.

Map of Consciousness (MOC). This David Hawkins' depiction of the levels of consciousness.

Numerical Sequence. IBFRT creates and imprints sequences of numbers of varying numbers of digits to magnify and specify a particular intention.

Remedy. A vial containing water that has been potentized homeopathically to a particular strength (potency) or imprinted through the power of intention.

Sarcode. A homeopathic remedy that is derived from an organ or tissue.

Schumann Resonance. A frequency that exists within the envelope between the surface of the earth and the ionosphere of about 7.39 hertz subject to many fluctuations and with other peaks too. Discovered by a German professor named Schumann, who studied the effects by living below the surface of the earth with the help of his students. The lack of exposure to this resonance is widely appreciated and sometimes referred to as geopathic stress. Changes to the atmosphere from natural or man-made activities affect the important regulatory influences of the resonance for human health. There is a great deal of information that the IBFRT practitioner is encouraged to explore through study, testing, and treatment.

Space Conditioning. Dr. William A. Tiller used the term "conditioned space" to describe the alteration of a physical space which was influenced by a positive intention from a device that delivered such an intention, as well as the effects of individuals and objects that manifested healing intentions. One important aspect of his work about space conditioning that is relevant to this book is that a conditioned space is a space which has a heightened ability to affect those who occupy it in a manner which facilitates increased love, peace, and healing.

Split or Splitting. Refers to an IBFRT response that is triggered through intention to reveal the presence of more than one incoherent condition.

Spiritual Gifts. IBFRT describes the "fruits of the Spirit" that are listed in Galatians 5:22-23 as the nine spiritual gifts. They are love, hopefulness, peacefulness, gentleness, faithfulness. Kindness, humility, self-control, and joy.

Two-Pointing. In the context of IBFRT only, it refers to that part of the "dog and pony show" when the practitioner determines that is helpful to employ an AK method to localize a stress (incoherence) with a particular body location for the purpose of demonstrating the connection between a particular incoherence and a bodily weakness, complaint, or symptom.

Upward Causation. The theory that the creation of all things begins at the physical level. Absolute everything, including that which does not appear to be physical, or measurable through a physical test or scientific experiment, is believed to come from a physical cause or source.

Whisperology. The theories that IBFRT uses to explain and develop its methods for testing and imprinting intention for the purpose of healing.

Yin Tang Point. An acupuncture point located midway between the medial ends of the eyebrows.

SUGGESTED READING

The interested reader may explore the theories of Whisperology, the tools of Whisperology Toolbox, and the use of Intention Based Field Resonance Testing (IBFRT) for testing and treatment by studying the following resources:

Required reading:
The Powers of Attention, Attraction, and Intention in Field Control Therapy, Intention Based Field Resonance Testing: The Power of the Whisper, Intention Based Field Resonance Testing: The Magnification of the Whisper, and *Intention Based Field Resonance Testing: The Geometry of the Whisper.* Written by Steven R Tonsager, MS., LAc., and founder of IBFRT.

Psychoenergetic Science: A Second Copernican-Scale Revolution. Written by Dr. William A. Tiller, Ph.D.

Bridging Science and Spirit: The Genius of William A. Tiller's Physics and the Promise of Information Medicine. Written by Dr. Nisha J. Manek, MD.

Power vs Force, Healing and Recovery, and *Letting Go* Written by Dr. David R Hawkins, MD., Ph.D.

Recommended reading:

The Dreams of EBKILFGN: An Allegory About Consciousness, *The Tales of EBKILFGN: An Allegory About Enlightenment*, and *The Return of EBKILFGN: An Allegory About Permanence*. Written by Steven R Tonsager, MS., LAc., and founder of IBFRT.

Science and Human Transformation. Subtle Energies and Human Transformation. Written by Dr. William A. Tiller, Ph.D. (Dr. Tiller's other books are highly recommended as well as the collection of his white papers, available on the Tiller Institute website at www.tillerfoundation.org.)

Deep Reality. Written by Dr. Doug Matzke, PhD. and Dr. William A Tiller, Ph.D. (A book that was written by Matzke, a computer scientist, incorporates many of Tiller's concepts into an imaginary conversation about what he calls "source science.")

The Eye of the I: From Which Nothing is Hidden, I: Reality and Subjectivity, and *Discovery Of The Presence of God: Devotional Nonduality.* Written by Dr. David R Hawkins, MD., PhD. (All of Dr. Hawkins' books are highly recommended.)

Made in United States
Cleveland, OH
05 March 2025